MW01688023

GARDENING IN SMALL SPACES

GARDENING IN SMALL SPACES

MARCUS SCHNECK

SHOOTING STAR PRESS

A QUINTET BOOK

This edition published in 1995 for:
Shooting Star Press, Inc.
230 Fifth Avenue, Suite 1212
New York, NY 10001

Copyright © 1992 Quintet Publishing Limited.
All rights reserved. No part of this publication may be reproduced, stored in a retrieval system or transmitted in any form or by any means, electronic, mechanical, photocopying, recording or otherwise, without the permission of the copyright holder.

ISBN 1-57335-297-7

Reprinted 1995

This book was designed and produced by
Quintet Publishing Limited
6 Blundell Street
London N7 9BH

Creative Director: Richard Dewing
Designer: James Lawrence
Editors: Stefanie Foster, Lindsay Porter
Illustrator: Danny McBride
Picture Researcher: Marcus Schneck

Typeset in Great Britain by
Central Southern Typesetters, Eastbourne
Manufactured in Singapore by
Bright Arts Pte Ltd
Printed in Singapore by
Star Standard Industries (Pte) Ltd

Contents

INTRODUCTION

FARMER'S MARKETS ARE WONDERful places. Stall after stall offer the freshest, tastiest produce to be had anywhere. Delectable vegetables of every variety cry out for space in the shopping basket. Knowledgeable local growers stand ready with advice on the best possible home-uses for their vegetables.

I know I'm not alone in this opinion. During the past decade or so, farmer's markets have sprung up from coast to coast, in nearly every community of any size that didn't already have one. And, the markets are flourishing. Shoulder-to-shoulder shoppers are the conditions I most often encounter whenever I drop in for a visit to the local farmer's market in whatever town I happen to be stopped in at the time. A good proportion of us clearly want the freshness and variety available at the farmer's market.

Although those markets will always be able to provide greater diversity – notably in fruits and nuts – each one of us can grow our own vegetable-version of the local farmer's market right in our garden, on our patio or in pots. With much less effort than might be expected we can even beat the freshest items that the farmer's market has to offer. Soil to table time can take just a few mintes, the time it takes to pick the vegetables, wash them off and combine them into whatever dish is being prepared.

And, we can do this almost everyday from late spring into autumn.

Huge garden plots are not needed to accomplish this feat. As a matter of fact, most home gardeners are currently using anywhere from 50 to 80 per cent more space than actually needed to produce their annual crops of vegetables. It follows that they also are using 50 to 80 per cent more labour and time, 50 to 80 per cent more fertilizers and other additives, 50 to 80 per cent more water, 50 to 80 per cent more money, 50 to 80 per cent more of nearly anything we might list that goes into the making of a garden.

▲ **Gargantuan garden plots are not necessary to grow most or all of the produce you will want or need from early spring through autumn. If you currently use conventional row-type gardening, the techniques presented here will cut the space you need by 50 to 80 per cent without reducing your harvest.**

We've all seen the results of this over-expenditure of resources, generally begun in late winter when the almost uncontrollable urge to do something outdoors combines with the pile of mail-order seed catalogues that have arrived over the past several months. Our mind's eye takes over at this point, clouding our planning and buying decisions with the image of huge expanses of lush greenery literally drenched in fresh edibles of every description.

By later summer that wonderful, enticing vision has run head-long into the harsh, cold world of reality. Those rows upon rows of courgette plants are overproducing to the point that friends and neighbours no longer answer the door when we come calling, generally with several of the over-sized marrows in tow. The dozen or so tomato plants are producing equally well, but threaten to topple under the weight at any minute if we don't get some additional stakes into their cages.

Weeds threaten to clog every inch of space where we don't knock them back at least weekly. Pest insects are having their way with whatever vegetable victim they choose.

For many the garden now becomes just too much work for the returns that it gives. More than a few gardens in any given neighbourhood at this time of the year are the sites of huge weed patches, stark testimony to the apparent victory of Nature over man. Where the rows are still maintained in a semblance of neatness and order, gardeners will find they are working over-time most evenings.

But, as I've pointed out, it doesn't have to be this way. It is possible to grow even more crops with much less bother. Conventional thinking about what a garden is, what a garden looks like and what goes into achieving that image is all that stands in the way of most gardeners.

▶ Much of what you're about to read is often nothing more than techniques that were practised by our ancestors, who relied much more heavily on their small kitchen gardens for the day-to-day necessities.

▼ Bountiful harvests, timed to coincide with your needs and tastes, are easily achieved by those who are willing to take a new approach to gardening.

Breaking through that conventional thinking is what this book is about. Hopefully by the time you reach the last page, you'll be able to look at your garden in an entirely new way.

With this new approach to gardening, you're going to have much richer, healthier soil. Every time you work in the garden, you'll be completing another step in the process of continuous soil improvement. In addition, you're going to be working anywhere from 50 to 80 per cent less garden space to produce the same amount of vegetables you now do in your much larger conventional row-type garden.

Your growing area will show a marked decrease in weed, pest and plant disease problems. Many of the techniques detailed throughout the book offer the side-benefit of reducing all three of these troublesome areas and ensuring earlier notice for you of any approaching concern.

And, your water needs are going to plummet. You're going to learn how to place every drop of water strategically to maximize its benefit to your plants. Even when drought-condition emergencies cause bans of garden watering, you'll find you have plenty of water to keep your garden in full production.

PLANNING WITH YOUR REAL NEEDS IN SIGHT

Have you ever purchased 40 radishes at one time? If you have, because of some special sale at the supermarket or for some similar reason, have you used them all before their quality had dropped below a level acceptable for further use?

Only the most rabid radish-lovers among us can honestly answer yes to both of these questions. For the rest of us, five or six snapping-crisp radishes downed with a side dish of buttered bread or diced into a fresh salad for variety are about all we want, and then only on occasion – definitely not every day.

So, why do so many of us plant an entire row of the vegetable each spring? Do we really enjoy seeing so many two-inch-diameter radishes, with woody texture and spicy hot taste beyond any reasonable uses, on the compost heap in early summer? Perhaps there's a sense of accomplishment in being able to bring so many individuals of one vegetable successfully to maturity? Or, maybe the seed packet told us to plant its contents at certain intervals in a row?

▲ **Use your likes and dislikes in making your decisions about what to plant, rather than the amazing photos on the seed packets or the incredible diversity available to you.**

◀ **How long would it take you to use 40 radishes? When you plant even a small number of seeds, like those in the palm of the hand in this photo, all at the same time, you're saying you will use them all in less than a week. Otherwise, they'll be left in the garden to become oversized and bitter like the specimen on the right.**

Start with your real needs and uses

Whatever our reasons, a much more productive approach to the radishes – and every other vegetable that we plant – is to start with some other criterion than how many seeds come in the packet or how much space our winter-crazed minds think we should devote to gaining some springtime greenery as soon as possible.

Look inside yourself rather than at these external clues. How many radishes – or courgettes, or tomatoes, or peppers, or whatever – do you generally use in a week? How many more might you use if they were readily available, both free and fresh, right through your back door?

These questions should be asked about every one of your favourite vegetables. That's right, your favourite vegetables, and only your favour-

◀ Plant what you like to eat. If you enjoy the taste of lettuce, for example, there are many, many varieties that you might try. 10 of them are shown growing in this raised bed.

ites. Why spend work, time, space and money on anything that you don't consider among your favourites' list? If you don't like radishes, or courgettes, or tomatoes, or peppers, or whatever, don't plant them.

Ask these questions about everything you want to plant before considering the size of your garden. Look ahead to what you will harvest and plan your garden based on that, rather than looking at the space you have available and planting that as full as possible.

For now, it's important not to think in terms of garden size. As you will see later, conventional thinking on this subject – the type of thinking you are likely to do at this point – won't serve any real purpose. We are redefining exactly what a garden is.

Plan your garden like you would plan your visit to the farmer's market, or as you would plan your visits there for the next six to eight months. Your grocery list, then, should be the real starting point in garden planning.

All this is not meant to imply that you will be able completely to replace your weekly trips to the market. Those gardeners who enter into this enterprise with the attitude that their upfront investment, both in effort and money, will result in enormous savings on future food bills are generally among those most disappointed with their crops and disillusioned with gardening. Unless they have the incredible amount of time required to produce and preserve such quantities of food, they are setting themselves up for a stressful endeavour.

You might see some savings down the line. But that is not the real benefit of gardening. The freshness, the control over what goes into at least some of your food, the variety – these are the real reasons for tilling the soil.

In addition to your favourite foods, you might want to include some of the latest varieties and exotic new discoveries offered by the seed cata-

▼ There might be some savings to be had from growing your own vegetables, but the real rewards are the experience and knowing exactly what is going into your food.

▲ **One real concern in planning the size of your garden must be how much work and time you are able to commit to it. Be realistic in your assessment.**

logues in your planning. The garden need not be an entirely serious endeavour, devoted 100 per cent to the production of your daily nourishment. There is plenty of room for experimentation, for special effort to bring off a particularly challenging species, for growing something just for the beauty it has to offer.

Your choice of what to plant and how much of it to plant must also be tempered by a realistic assessment of the time you can, and will, devote to the garden. For example, later chapters will outline special efforts that make growing and harvesting much earlier in the spring and much later in the fall completely feasible. But they are special efforts and require some extra effort and time. If you can't commit to that extra effort and time, don't plan for the additional harvests. Admitting that you have other activities in your life that preclude that commitment to the garden is not some sign of a deep-seated character flaw. Instead, it's an indication that you have thought out the process in a realistic manner and made some balanced decisions.

Onto the catalogues

With your "grocery list" in hand, it's time to pull that growing pile of seed catalogues, which have been arriving for months now, from the magazine rack. Follow your list as you make your selections, using the information in the catalogues to choose those varieties that are best suited to your region and your tastes.

Your most troubling effort at this time of year will be resisting the urge to over-buy. As you leaf through page after page of lush spring and summer growth, with the winter wind howling across a snow-covered landscape outside, your urge for outdoor activity and warmer weather will be quite strong. Don't permit that urge, those desires, to make your buying decisions.

Remember, one of the focuses of this book is to reduce the space you need to commit to garden by 50 to 80 per cent. You simply won't need as many packets of seeds as you did previously. In most instances, unless you adapt the techniques of this book to much larger scale gardening than we propose here, you won't use all the seeds in any of the packets you do buy.

Another urge you're likely to feel will come from the wonderful photos that the catalogues use to portray the results of the seeds they offer. Don't let the brilliant colours and delectable arrangements add too many additional vegetable types to your shopping list. Remember, you developed that list based on the types you like to eat, the types you generally do eat, the types you're likely to actually use from the garden.

Seed Catalogues

Ordering from seed catalogues can give us a much needed boost during the house-bound days of mid-winter, but there is a much more serious reason for buying from these national suppliers. As you will see later, the conditions under which seeds are stored determine how well the seeds will germinate and sprout in the garden. The national suppliers have perfected those storage conditions that give their customers the best possible seeds. Otherwise they wouldn't be in the business for very long. In most instances, the same cannot be said of the local garden centre or department store.

If you want to patronize local businesses, everything else you will need for gardening can be purchased there. But, for your seeds, rely on the national catalogue companies.

▲ Storage conditions are crucial to how well the seeds you buy will germinate and sprout. For this reason, it's generally safer to buy your seeds from the mail-order catalogues.

For some of the vegetable types you've included on your list, you'll find upwards of two dozen varieties offered in some of the larger catalogues. Read the description carefully. In general, avoid the extra large varieties of any vegetable that does not grow on a vine. While such super-size pepper or aubergine plants will often grow the larger fruits as promised, the plants will probably take up an equally larger amount of your gardening space.

By choosing the smaller, normal varieties you will be able to grow more plants in the same amount of space and, in nearly all cases, will realize significantly more fruits and a larger overall harvest as a result.

For some vegetables there simply is no way around devoting large spaces to their growth. Courgettes are our best example. They're a staple of almost every garden. And, they do produce a fulfillingly large harvest. But one plant will eat up anywhere from 8 to 16 square feet of garden space. That's a lot of productive ground devoted to just one type of vegetable. On top of that, how many courgettes can you really eat? Whole books have been written on the search for more uses for the prolific produce.

If you really love courgettes you will want to devote the necessary space to the raising of it. On the other hand, if your need is simply for marrow, there are many varieties that will do very nicely when grown vertically over much less total ground space. We'll be discussing vertical growing in detail later on, but for now you need to know that you have this option when you make your seed selections.

Buy the indeterminate varieties of all trailing crops, such as tomatoes, marrow and melon.

▲ Indeterminate varieties of vining crops, such as tomatoes, are preferred for vertical growing methods that maximise small space. These varieties grow in long vines, while the determinate varieties grow into short bushes.

These varieties grow in long trails, while the determinate varieties grow into short bushes. For the important vertical growth techniques we'll discuss later, this is a crucial buying decision.

When making your decisions about beans, choose the climbing varieties. Not only are they intended for vertical growth, the climbing varieties generally produce their harvest over a more sustained period of time.

Ignoring some "expert" advice

Several weeks after you place your order with the seed companies, those wonderful fact-filled packets will begin to arrive. The accumulated knowledge of these ages, as it relates to each specific vegetable variety, will be presented on the packets. Everything you need to know to grow that vegetable successfully is detailed there, often in vivid colour and graphics.

If you follow the instructions exactly, most often you will grow a crop of perfectly fine vegetables. You will also waste a lot of garden space, water, time and effort.

Although this is slowly changing, most of the techniques presented on the seed packets are the result of research and practice in commercial agriculture. In addition to the questionable use of pesticides, herbicides and all sorts of other "-cides" by much of the commercial agriculture community today, there is another huge difference from the type of gardening we plan to do. Commercial agriculture, dependent on large machines to achieve its profit margins, must have the large spaces between rows for those machines to operate.

This is the reason that most seed packet instructions allow much closer spacing within the row than between rows. For example, one commonly available variety of New Zealand spinach suggests a spacing of 12 in (30 cm) between plants but 24 in (60 cm) between rows. On the other hand, the spinach listing in our directory of plants at the back of this book suggests 4 in (10 cm) of space on all sides of the plant.

With the techniques you'll discover in later chapters of this book, you won't need the wide paths for moving between your rows. And, with-

▲ Traditional row-type gardening that 90 percent of gardeners currently use is largely based on the practices and needs of commercial agriculture.

The machinery needs of commercial agriculture are one of the reasons that your seed packets tell you to allow large paths between rows.

out the compaction that such traffic would cause between the rows, the plants won't need the extra space either. In addition, even the in-row spacing of plants suggested on most seed packets is much too conservative and totally out of place in the intensive gardening techniques you will be using from this point forward.

(NOTE • Read the last four paragraphs several times again. The close spacing of intensive gardening is one of the most important techniques for making your garden produce more for every foot of space.)

The seed packet will also tell you to plant three seeds for New Zealand spinach at those intervals and then go back when the three seedlings that sprout are about 2 in (5 cm) tall and thin to just one seedling. Such precautions are primarily for the benefit of the seed company's reputation.

That packet contains good seeds that have been preserved under perfect conditions. Just about every single seed in that packet is going to germinate and sprout. But the seed company wants to make sure you have a positive impression of their product, so they're telling you to give them this extra margin for success.

Break out of this trap. Plan to plant just one seed at the spacing suggested later in this book. As a matter of fact, planting just one seed at each location is another of the basic tenets of the gardening technique we're presenting here, for nearly all types of vegetables. It's one of our labour-saving techniques: you won't need to do any thinning. Try it. I think you'll be pleasantly surprised.

The rest of the information on the seed packet can be taken at face-value. The seed companies have your best interests at heart. They want you to buy from them again next year, and the year after that, and the year after that, and so on. However, the information we've just discussed needs to be updated for today's gardener.

▲ If you want and enjoy a large garden, feel free to have a large garden. The techniques presented in this book adapt just fine. But be prepared for an incredible harvest.

◄ Apart from ensuring the reputation of the seed company, there really is very little reason to plant three seeds and then thin-out the two extras when all three sprout.

Choosing your optimum garden size

With seed packets in hand and grocery lists of what you want to eat from the garden nearby, you are ready to determine how much space you need to commit to the amount of produce you want. Begin by sorting the packets into three stacks:

– Those vegetables that trail. You will be growing these vertically and realizing the greatest saving in garden space ever developed.

– The warm-season summer vegetables.

– Those vegetables that can be planted outdoors before the last springtime frost.

Now take a look at the space you have available to work with. If you have one rectangular plot of ground that you want to commit to gardening, as gardeners have done in conventional row-type planting for generations, that's fine – although we mostly won't be using it for rows.

But, if you don't have that type of space or don't want to commit that space to gardening, that's equally fine. Throughout this book we will use the term "garden" to mean any space that you have designated for that use. It might be a 24-sq in (60 sq cm) space at the base of a bird table or rotary clothes drier where you want to plant a tomato. It might be the 6-in (15-cm) wide strip along a fence that you plan to use for several varieties of beans. It might be a series of large pots that you will place about your patio, one with a tomato plant, another with a pepper plant, and so on. Or it might be the conventional, rectangular garden. In our definition, all these are a garden.

The most crucial consideration in garden size – no matter what description fits your garden – is your relationship to those dimensions. No segment of your garden should be more of a reach than two feet from the outside of the plot. In other words, no section of the garden should be more than two feet from the edge of your garden. This is the distance that most of us can cover with the reach of our arms, without having to lean or step onto the garden soil at all.

If you plan a much larger plot, plan it in 4-ft (122-cm)-wide segments with paths of at least 2 ft (60 cm) between each segment. For example, if you have a 10-by-20-ft (3m-by-6m) plot for your garden, plan it as two segments 4 ft (122 cm) wide by 20 ft (6 m) long with a 2-ft (60 cm)-wide path down the centre.

▼ By laying out your garden in plots that are no more than 4 feet wide, with 2-foot-wide paths between, you will be able to reach all areas of the garden without stepping or leaning on the garden soil. Climbing crops and taller plants should be placed at the northern exposure of the garden so they don't overshadow shorter plants.

PLOT LAYOUT

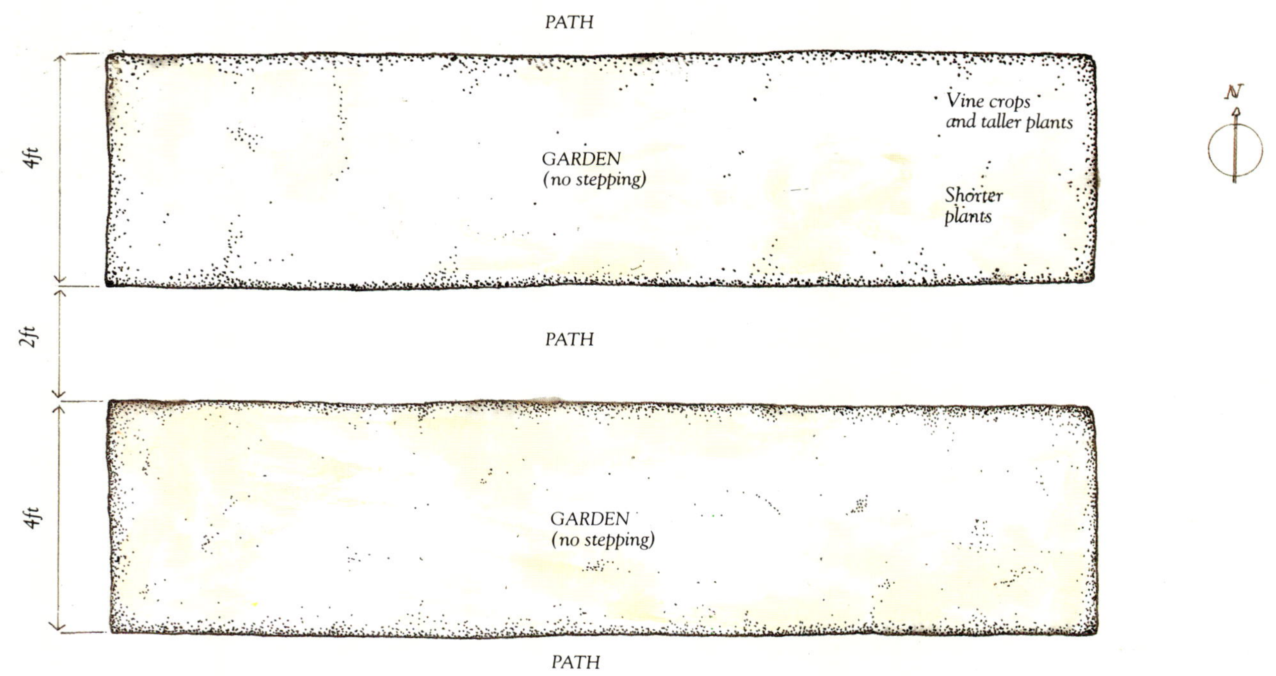

We leave this extra, non-producing space to provide a buffer against compaction of the soil. If we were to walk on the soil, or even lean on it, we would compact the particles that make it up into a much denser arrangement. The more we walked on the soil, the more we would compact it. And, the more compacted the soil becomes the less it permits much needed air and water to penetrate the roots of our crops.

This is the underlying reason why nearly every gardening book, including this one, warns against working in wet soil early in spring. The same compaction takes place and is magnified under those conditions.

Begin your planning with the trailing crops. You will be growing these vertically and, thus,

▲ **You don't need to be locked into the typical mega-sized rectangular garden any longer. The same amount of food, even more, can be grown on much less space.**

▼ **The most critical siting/sizing decision you will make involves the outer dimensions of each plot in your garden. You should be able to reach and work every inch of the entire garden without ever walking on the garden itself.**

► **Make paths around your garden plots and stick to them. Every time you step on your garden soil you compact that soil and lose some more of the friability shown here in this cut-away of a radish plot.**

need to place them along the northernmost part of your garden to prevent the shading of other, shorter crops. Use the plant descriptions at the back of this book to plan for spacing.

Next, plan spaces for the warm-season summer crops. These plants take the maximum amount of time to grow and produce their crops, and will need to occupy their spacing for nearly the entire growing season.

However, it is possible to get an additional crop from each of these spaces by planting a faster-growing vegetable at the edges. This temporarily makes use of the extra space that the warm-season plant will eventually need but does not yet occupy. For example, peppers need to be spaced at 12 in (30 cm), but that's at maturity. When the young transplant is first placed in the garden, about two weeks after the last spring frost, it will take up only 4 in (10 cm) or so at the centre of the space. Even before that tender warm-season plant is placed there, you could have harvested a full crop of lettuce from the space. And, when the pepper is planted, another crop of lettuce could be grown around the edges of the space before the pepper needs the full area.

Finally, in whatever space remains, plan for your cooler season crops. Using the succession techniques we will discuss later, you will be able to grow two or three crops each spring-early summer on each one of these spaces.

Selecting the garden site

With the conventional row-type definition of a garden now behind us, we have much more latitude in our choice of garden sites. No longer must we find a large enough spot to hold the entire garden *en masse*. No longer does the sheer size of the garden dictate that it is placed as far away from the house and lawn as possible.

About the only siting criterion that matters any longer is sunlight. We can adjust the other factors that govern plant growth: soil and water. But our location and local environment pretty much dictate what we have to work with in terms of the amount of sunlight available.

This is one area where plants are very unforgiving. They need just as many hours of sunlight every day as you can possible scrounge for them. Without adequate sunlight, warm-season crops such as tomatoes will produce a severely limited crop. At a minimum our plants need six hours per day, and eight is much better. In addition, the optimum sunlight for growing generally occurs between 9 am and 4 pm.

A southern exposure is always preferred over exposure in any of the other three directions. This is the direction from which the fullest rays of sunlight will come, and the entire garden should be planned to take the fullest advantage of that fact. It is for this reason that we plan our garden starting with the vertically grown, tallest crops to the north and progressively shorter crops towards the south. In this way we don't shade any crop with the one next to it.

Of course, some crops actually do better in some shade. For example, four to six hours of sunlight per day is plenty for beetroot, carrots, cauliflower, Swiss chard, cucumbers, lettuce, onions, parsley, peas, radishes, spinach and marrows. In the hottest, sunniest days of summer, these crops may actually need some shade.

Everything by the calendar

With the garden planned out, you next need to turn to the calendar. A large wall-type calendar is needed, the type that shows an entire month on a page and allows space for you to jot in your own notes on each day.

Use the frost maps in Appendix A of this book to determine the date of the last spring frost in your area. You will notice that these are large-scale maps covering large areas within each of the regions they designate.

Continual Varied Harvesting From a Small Plot

The same bit of ground that will grow a warm-season plant, such as a pepper in this example, can also be used to grow several crops of cool-season plants, such as salad bowl lettuce in this example. All of the soil can be used for the cool-season plants before the warm-season plant is placed there. Much of the soil can be used for cool-season plants while the warm-season plant is growing. All of the soil can be used for the cool-season plants again in the autumn after the warm-season plant has been harvested.

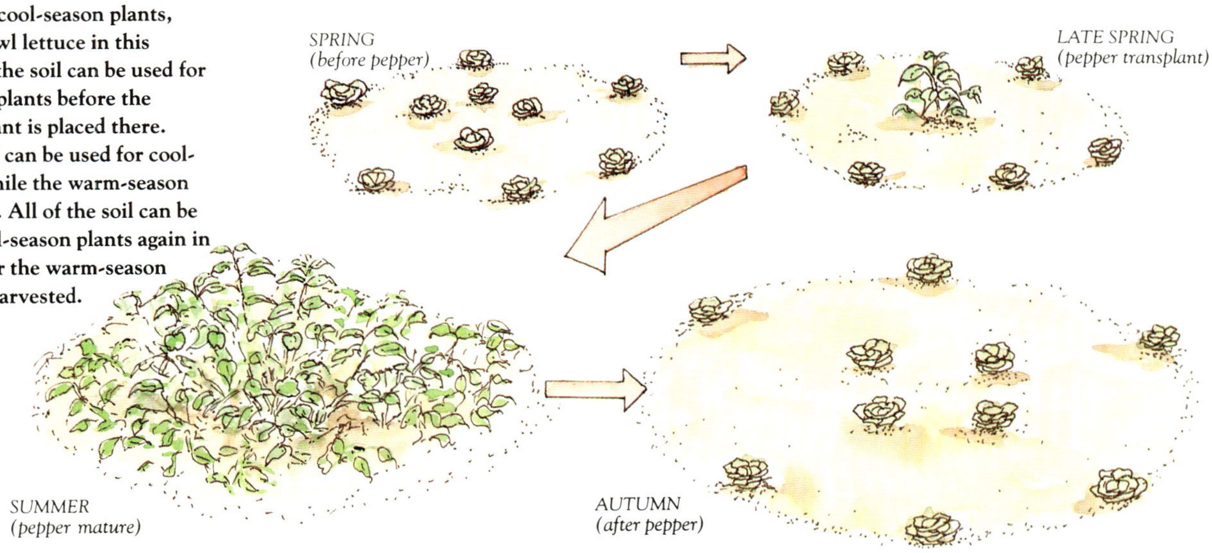

VEGETABLE	SUNLIGHT REQUIREMENTS					
	1hr	2hrs	3hrs	4hrs	5hrs	6hrs
ASPARAGUS						
AUBERGINE						
BEANS						
BEETROOT						
BROCCOLI						
BRUSSELS SPROUTS						
CABBAGE						
CARROTS						
CAULIFLOWER						
CHIVES						
CUCUMBERS						
ENDIVE						
GARLIC						
KALE						
KOHLRABI						
LEEKS						
LETTUCE						
MARROW						
MUSTARD						
ONIONS						
PARSLEY						
PEAS						
PEPPERS						
RADISHES						
SPINACH						
SWEETCORN						
SWISS CHARD						
TOMATOES						
TURNIPS						
	PARTIAL SUN (4 HOURS PER DAY)				FULL SUN (6+ HOURS PER DAY)	

This is fine general advice and will hold true, but variations from these dates of as much as two weeks either way have been noted. To make a more precise estimate on the last spring frost for your specific locale, you might want to make a phone call to your local meteorological office or talk to some long-time gardeners in your neighbourhood. You might find that the last frost comes a few weeks earlier or later than the maps at the back of this book portray. In which case, mark whatever date you determine as your last-spring-frost date on the calendar.

Now, using the individual plant listings at the back of this book, find each of the crops that you have planned for your garden and determine their appropriate planting dates – starting seeds indoors, starting seeds outdoors and transplanting to the outdoors – in relation to the last-spring-frost date. Note down each of these dates on the calendar as well.

Place the calendar in some spot around the house where you are sure to see it every day. And, make it your daily concern to check to see if you're on schedule. Don't push yourself to the point of fanaticism about the schedule. That will only dampen your interest in your garden. But, try to stay on schedule to maximize the growing time your garden can offer.

GROWING UP, AS WELL AS OUT

ANY TRAILING CROP CAN BE grown vertically just as well, usually better, as it can be grown horizontally along the ground. Every trailing plant grown vertically represents a substantial increase in per-square-foot harvest.

Not only will the vertically grown plant take up less garden space, but it will gain better access to sunlight and air circulation. It will generally be prone to less insect and disease damage, because it will be easy for you to spot and correct any developing problems almost before they start. And, it will mean less bending over for you. You'll be tending a crop that stands much closer to eye-level.

This is another of the crucial basic concepts that we want you to take away from this book. Among other crops, it applies to beans, cucumbers, melons (including cantaloupes), peas, courgettes and marrows and tomatoes – or, as you can see, many of our favourite garden vegetables. We cause these trailing crops to grow up rather than out by providing them with a variety of vertical supports and attaching them to those supports.

▼ **Vertically grown crops offer easier access every time you need to work with them or near them. They also have better access to sunlight and improved air circulation.**

DIFFERENT TYPES OF SUPPORTS FOR VERTICAL GROWING OF A TRAILING CROP

Several support designs have been developed for growing trailing crops vertically. As with most gardening techniques, "the simpler the better" is a good guideline here. Simple tomato cages and wooden poles have performed well for generations of gardeners.

1 Circular wire cage

2 Wooden pole

◀ Stakes are another alternative for supporting your vertical crops.

▼ Commercially available tomato cages, 5 or 6 ft (1.5–2 m) tall, provide fine support for your vertical crops. They probably will need a stake or two to remain stable when the plant is full-grown and the crop is heavy.

3 Frame of metal pipes with string

4 Garden fence

► Some systems employ twine or rope hung from an overhead frame of metal pipes or wooden boards as support for vertical crops. The strings can cut into the plant stems when they're hanging full of crops later in the season.

The tomato cages sold at almost every garden centre are one very adequate method for supporting this vertical growth. Until recently the tallest cages generally available were 4 ft (1.22 m) high, but in recent years 5- and even 6-footers have been available. The taller, the better – up to 6 ft (1.83 m) should be your guiding axiom in choosing all vertical supports.

You can make your own cages from fence wire by looping a section in a circle of 2- (60 cm) to 3-ft (90 cm) in diameter. Use wire with openings of about 4-by-6 in (10-by-15 cm) to allow access.

The one drawback with cages, which several authors have been quick to point out, is their need for additional support. If cages are your choice – and they are a very good choice – plan to hold them in place and steady with wooden or metal stakes driven a couple of feet into the ground. Generally no more than two such stakes are needed for each cage. Be sure to drive the stakes into the ground before you plant whatever crop will be using the cages, so as to avoid damage to the plant's roots.

Stakes are another totally adequate method for supporting your vertical crops. Some authors have complained that wooden stakes tend to split and break by season end, but I have not found this to be the case unless inadequate wood was used in the first place. Metal stakes are another option. Again, be certain to drive the stakes several feet into the ground, leaving 6 ft (1.22 m) protruding aboveground, before you plant your crop.

► The tee-pee type arrangements so often popular for growing beans will serve just as well for any crops that are grown vertically. They are very stable.

The guideline that my family has used for generations in using stakes and cages is this: for fewer but larger tomatoes use poles; for more but smaller tomatoes use cages. It generally applies to all vertical crops.

A variation on the stake method is to arrange three or four poles in a tee-pee arrangement or to extend three or four strong ropes from the top of a stake to tent-type stakes on the ground in this same array. Plant at the base of each of the downward slanting supports.

Yet another vertical support system involves a frame of metal pipes built so that about 7 ft (2.10 m) protrudes aboveground and several feet vertical pipes have been driven into the ground. From the top crosspiece that connects the two vertical pipes, which should never be more than 6 ft (1.83 m) apart, strong string or fence wire is hung down to about a foot off the ground. We don't take the string or wire all the way to the ground so that we have space to work unobstructed at the base of the plant all the time.

Again, if fence wire is used it should have openings of at least 4-by-6 in (10-by-15 cm) to allow you to get your hands inside to work at the plant. It should also be attached securely to the vertical pipes at both sides. If string is used it should be attached at the bottom – about a foot above ground – to a horizontal strip of the same string attached to the two vertical pipes.

A fourth type of vertical support that you might consider is whatever structure you may already have in your garden. Bird table poles, washing line poles, fences, railings, etc., all will provide fine support for your vertical crops. Just be sure that there isn't too much people-traffic too close to such structures for the plant to reach maturity and bear its fruit.

The only soil you will need to prepare at the base of each vertical structure is the space described under spacing in the plant directory. For example, each broad bean plant needs 6–8 in (15–20 cm) of soil space. That's all you'll need to prepare, using the soil preparation techniques we'll describe later, for the plant to reach its full potential. If you decide to plant a broad bean plant to grow up each of the four main legs of a tomato cage, you need only prepare 6–8 sq in (15–20 sq cm) of soil at each of the four legs.

Similarly, only the space immediately surrounding the plant will need to be watered.

As the plants grow, most will need to be physically attached to the support every 6 in (15 cm) or so. Strips torn from old T-shirts or similarly soft material and tied loosely about the support and the plant stem fulfil this function without cutting into the plant stem's outer wall. String, twine, rope and rubbish bag wire closures generally cannot make this claim.

If using a stake or the vertical frame method with string, the plant should constantly be pruned back to only the main stem. With cages of fence wire, the main stem and a couple of additional side stems should be allowed, but all others should be pruned. This forces all the growth potential coursing from the plant's roots to channel into that single stem or those few stems. Growth that would have occurred on additional side stems is lost, but it is more than compensated for in the more vigorous, earlier-ripening growth on the remaining stem or stems. This strict pruning also holds the plant's growth into the tight growing limits essential to maximum yield from every square foot of garden space.

The pruning should begin sometime in June. On tomato plants completely prune off the suckers, the extra stems that appear in the angle between each leaf stem and the main stem (from the same spot where the leaf stem emerged), an inch or so from the main stem. For marrow and melons, pluck the light-green, fuzz-covered growing tips from the plants that emerge from the main stem. Pruning is not necessary in the case of cucumbers and beans.

As the plant reaches the top of its vertical support, which optimally is 6 ft (1.83 m) above ground, simply prune off all additional growth. If you allow the plant to continue growing beyond this point, there is a very good chance that the additional growth will be wasted when the above-support growth becomes too heavy and snaps off the stem.

The plant's reaction to this pruning will be to send off additional side-stems further down on the main stem. If this occurs in early August, you might want to allow a few of the extra stems to continue growing and set their fruit. However, if it happens in September, you will want to prune it off to force all growing power of the plant into ripening the fruit it has already set before the first frost of autumn.

Vertically grown marrow and melons generally will provide plenty of support for their fruits on their own. But I've always enjoyed the peace of mind that comes with further protecting the fruits from unexpected falls from the plant by enclosing them in loose nylon stocking ends, very loose nylon mesh bags or slings made of T-shirt material attached to the vertical support system. It's a bit more work, but I haven't lost any marrow or melons to a quick smashing on the ground. You decide what's right for your garden.

▲ With most vertical support systems you will need physically to attach the plant to the support. Strips of old T-shirt material are strong, but soft enough not to damage the stems they hold in place.

◀ Cucumber plants generally do not need to be pruned at any time during the season. Each plant will produce fruits. It's more important with cucumbers to pick the fruit before it grows too large.

SUCCESSION PLANTING

THOSE OF US WHO WANT TO maximize harvest on every square foot of garden space, follow yet another maxim religiously: never allow any part of the garden to remain unproductive during the growing season, but plant so that your harvest coincides with the timing of your needs.

Succession planting is the term to cover this philosophy. It has two components:

– Immediately after a crop is harvested from a given space in the garden, the soil in that space is refurbished and a new crop is planted.

– Every crop is planted so that only as much of it as we need or want at any given time is ready for harvest.

This stands in marked contrast to the conventional row-type garden, where nearly all the space is used to produce just one crop per year and each crop comes to harvestable maturity all at once. Remember the last time you had a dozen mega-sized courgettes to pawn off on friends and neighbours as a result of this?

The first step to successful succession planting is to plan for the continued use of and spread-out harvest from each space in your garden. You might approach this in a very formal manner, charting out the use for each space on graph paper or a calendar. You might also come at it from a much less formal angle, making your succession decisions as the gardening season progresses.

Regardless of the approach that suits you best, here is how it works, using lettuce, radishes and tomatoes as our example vegetables. We'll assume that we enjoy eating all three of these and want them in as continuous a supply as possible over as long a period as possible.

As we discussed in our chapter on planning, begin with the long-standing, warm-season crop: the tomato plant. You won't want to place the tomato seedling outside until the predicted date of the last spring frost. The spacing for the tomato plant is 24 in (60 cm), two feet that would be wasted until well into summer if it wasn't used for other purposes in advance of the tomato.

By contrast, radishes can be planted outside four weeks before the date of the last frost, they

▲ For maximum yield, every inch of your garden should remain in production throughout the growing season. Refurbish the soil and replant just as soon after each harvest as possible.

VEGETABLE	OPTIMUM SPACING (IN INCHES)											
	2	4	6	8	10	12	14	16	18	20	22	24
ASPARAGUS												
BEANS (BROAD)												
BEANS (RUNNER)												
BEANS (FRENCH)												
BEETROOT												
BROCCOLI												
BRUSSELS SPROUTS												
CABBAGE												
CARROTS												
CAULIFLOWER												
CHIVES												
COLLARDS (KALE PLAIN–LEAVED)												
CUCUMBERS												
EGGPLANT (AUBERGINE)												
ENDIVE												
GARLIC												
KALE (CURLY–LEAVED)												
KOHLRABI												
LEEKS												
LETTUCE (HEAD)												
LETTUCE (SALAD BOWL)												
MARROW												
MUSTARD												
ONIONS												
PARSLEY												
PEAS												
PEPPERS												
RADISHES												
SPINACH												
SWEETCORN												
SWISS CHARD												
TOMATOES												
TURNIPS												

◀ Traditional row-type spacing requirements, which call for more space between rows than between plants in the same row, can be discarded under the small scale gardening methods. Plants can be placed closer together than those traditional distances both in the row and row-to-row.

Radishes and salad bowl lettuce are fast growers that can be planted very early in the spring. Tomatoes, on the other hand, are slow growers that must be planted in the warmer weather. Using this knowledge, it's possible to harvest at least two crops of radishes and one of lettuce from the space intended for tomatoes, before the tomato has even been planted in the garden. Another, albeit smaller, crop of lettuce can be had from the edges of the same space while the tomato plant is growing there.

▲ **Members of the mustard family, including cabbage, broccoli and cauliflower, should be rotated from one space in the garden to another with every new planting. This discourages diseases that remain in the soil to which they are susceptible.**

require only four weeks to reach harvest size and they can be planted only 3 in (7 cm) apart. We could plant the entire 24 sq in (60 sq cm) of tomato space with 32 radishes four weeks before the last frost and harvest all 32 radishes when we plant the tomato. But 32 radishes would be too many to eat all at once.

Lettuce takes about seven weeks to reach maturity from the planting of the seed and we can start the seeds indoors eight weeks before the last frost, moving the transplants outside four weeks later. The same tomato space of 24 sq in (60 sq cm) would be capable of providing for 16 lettuce plants, harvested one week after the last frost. But again that would be too much lettuce all at once, and we couldn't plant the middle of the space because we want that for the tomato seedling on the date of the last frost.

Using succession on this small plot of ground, we can plant nine radish seeds spaced at 3-in (7-cm) intervals in the centre of the space and transplant eight lettuce seedlings around the outside of the space four weeks before the last frost. We'll be harvesting lettuce leaves about a week before it's time to plant the tomato and can continue leaf-by-leaf harvest for several weeks more. We'll have nine radishes ready for harvest when the weather is ready for the tomato seedlings to go

We can repeat the process along the southern-exposure, outside edges of the tomato space at the other end of the season by planting a line of lettuce seeds or seedlings about eight weeks before the predicted date of the first autumn frost. The tomatoes will continue to ripen for harvest, while a new crop of lettuce will grow at their "feet".

Succession also refers to the staggered planting of one crop in one space at different time intervals. For example, a square foot will grow 16 radishes. If we planted them all at once, in about four weeks we would have 16 radishes demanding to be harvested before they grow too large and sharp-tasting. For most of us that would be too many to eat within a few days. The solution is to plant some of the seeds, perhaps half, now and the rest in one week. The resulting harvest will be eight one week followed by eight the next, amounts that we can enjoyably consume at their peak of freshness.

(NOTE • The listings in the plant directory at the back of this book provide a staggered planting rotation for all of the crops to which this latter succession method can be applied.)

To continue succession throughout as much of the growing season as possible, you need to act as soon as any space becomes available anywhere in the garden. Right after harvesting the last of the crop on a given space, remove all of its stems and leaves, add an appropriate amount of fertilizer mix (explained later) to the soil and plant your next crop.

In succession planting never plant the same type of crop again in a space immediately after itself. This is known as crop rotation. To ignore it is to invite disaster: not only will this lead to faster depletion of the nutrients from the soil because the same type of crop will naturally need the same type nutrients, but it is one of the quickest ways to invite disease organisms onto the site. Members of the nightshade family, such as aubergines and tomato, and of the mustard family, such as broccoli and cabbage, are particularly susceptible.

Even if you don't practise succession planting, you will want to observe crop rotation from year to year. For these same reasons, you won't want to have broccoli growing on the same spot two years in a row.

Succession planting naturally results in succession harvesting. Rather than waiting for all of a given crop to be ready for harvest in one big gathering at one time, we now can harvest daily. The greens, radishes, carrots and such needed for a garden salad can be taken almost every day, combined later in the season with our own toma-

Traditional Row-type Methods

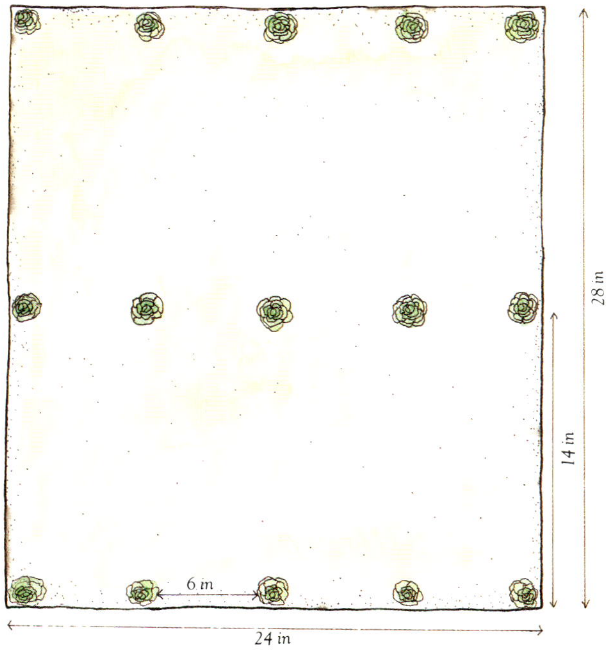

Small Space Gardening Methods

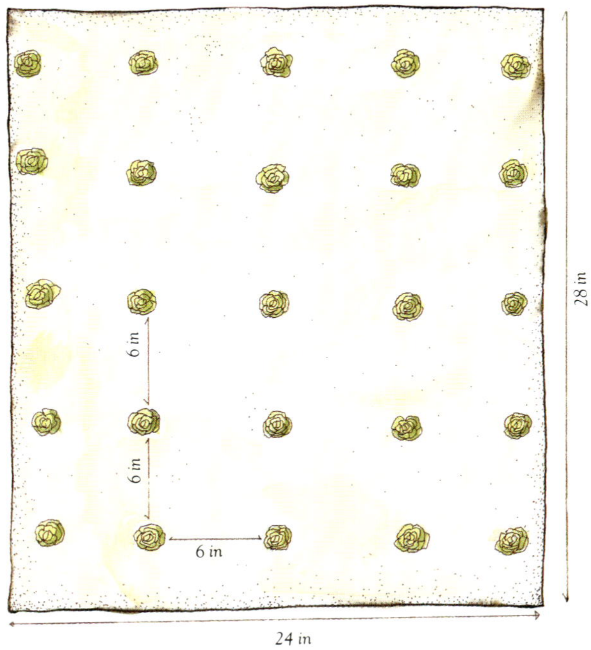

Small space gardening techniques can bring about a much larger harvest on the same amount of garden space, or a similarly sized harvest on a much reduced amount of garden space. In this example, the same 24-by-28-in (70-by-70 cm) garden space will grow 15 salad bowl lettuce plants under traditional row-type methods, or 45 salad bowl lettuce plants under small space gardening techniques.

Crop Rotation

By shifting the different families of plants, crop rotation helps to ensure that each new planting will have the nutrients it needs available for its use and that diseases don't spread from one planting to the next through the soil.

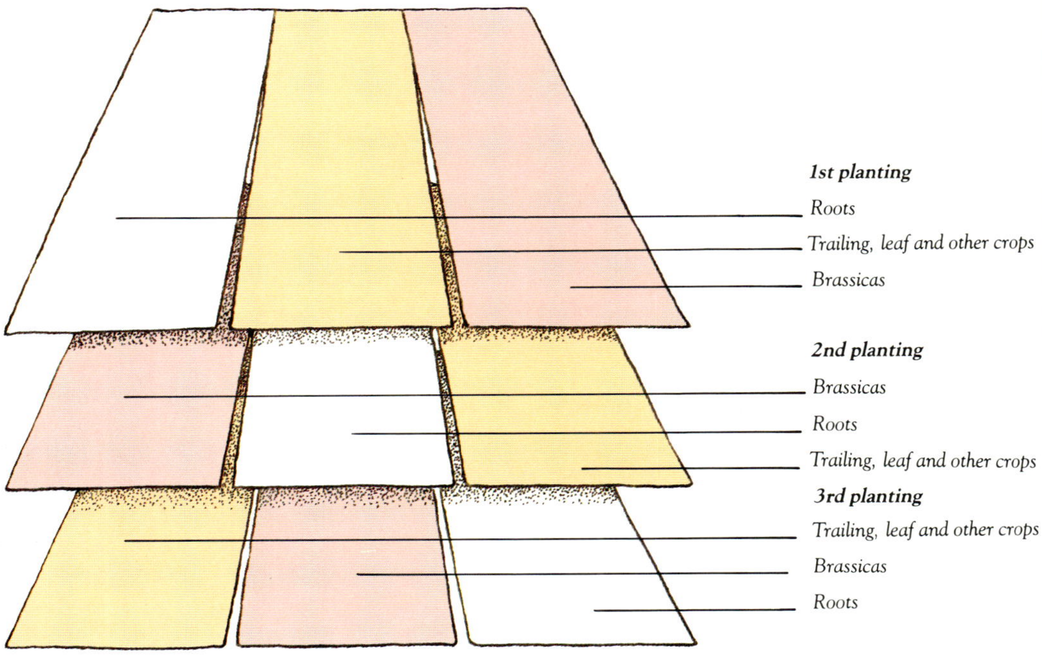

toes, peppers and the like. Two or three times a week we will find some crop ready for harvest and use in some side dish or main course.

To make the most of such wonderful, long-term bounty we must get into the routine of visiting the garden nearly every day just to determine what's ready or nearly ready for harvest and plan our meals accordingly. To me, this sounds a great deal like shopping at a farmer's market.

This new attitude also should think of freshness in our vegetables in terms of hours from garden to table. Vegetables begin a losing battle for freshness the minute they are picked, even when refrigerated. But, with our new way of harvesting, we can help them a great deal in that fight.

We are in essence turning back the calendar on gardening to the days when our pioneer ancestors relied on their small kitchen patches for much of their daily food. As soon as something was ready to eat that's exactly what was done with it, and nothing wasted.

We also won't want to let any of our crops continue growing too long. We should no longer think in terms of the vegetable size offered at the supermarket, or even at the farmer's market. Those crops have been grown to and beyond maturity with a single focus on impressive size. They generally passed the growth stage much earlier, well before they had achieved this size.

Harvesting when vegetables are about half the size we've been conditioned to expect will render the best taste and tenderest texture. Such "early"

▲ Visit the garden daily to see what's ready or nearly ready for harvest and plan your meals accordingly.

► Vegetable quality begins to deteriorate the moment the crop is removed from the plant. The sooner you can get it on the table after picking, the better the taste and texture.

▲ **Many vegetables, particularly beans, cucumbers, peas and marrow, are much better eaten when picked at about half-grown stages. Try this with courgettes for a really pleasant surprise.**

harvest will often cause the plant to produce yet an additional crop. When peas, marrow, beans, aubergines or cucumbers are picked at an early stage, the plant will continue to send out blossoms followed by fruit over a much longer period. Lettuce and spinach will continue to produce new leaves to replace those that have been taken. Broccoli will generate new side-shoots to replace the main head when it's removed.

Root crops, such as beetroot and carrots, won't generate additional growth after harvest, but the taste of the "half-grown" crops will be beyond compare.

The tools you'll need

You may already have reached the conclusion on your own that you won't need nearly as many tools to fully implement this intensive form of gardening. And, unless you plan to adapt our techniques for much larger than average garden needs, this is certainly true.

At a minimum: a shovel or spade will be needed for turning the soil and mixing in the enhancements and nutrients that we will explain later. A trowel will be needed for in-season soil work. A large bucket and some sort of handheld container will be needed for watering. A pair of secateurs is a nice addition to make a cleaner, healthier job of pruning the vertically grown crops.

In addition, we'll outline some other items that you may or may not want to add to your arsenal beyond the few simple tools we've mentioned here. It's really up to you.

► **The tools necessary for small space gardening are quite minimal: along with a bucket all work in the small-space garden can be fully accomplished with these few tools.**

Garden Tools

A DEEPER UNDERSTANDING OF YOUR SOIL

When we think of gardening the image that generally comes to mind is the lush green plants packed to capacity with fresh, firm crops. Rarely does such an initial vision include an image of the soil in which those crops are growing.

But this is truly a cart-before-the-horse situation. The plants and crops are the result of the soil. Without adequate soil they wouldn't even exist. And, the better the soil, the better the plants fare and the larger the production of crops. Soil is the aspect of gardening where we can have our greatest impact on our eventual harvest and therefore warrants a particular and in-depth understanding.

Where crops begin

Your first consideration must be whether the soil is ready to be worked. When you make a fist around a handful of the soil, does it drip water? If so, it's too wet. This is most often the condition in early spring. Does it form a ball, but fall apart when poked with a finger? Then it's ready for working. Won't it form a ball at all? Then it's too dry, although it can be worked quite easily.

The fist test can also tell us what type of soil we're dealing with. Soil is a collection of various particles, organic and mineral, separated by microscope passageways. We would be much more accurate to say that our plant's roots grow **between** the soil – in these passageways – rather than **in** the soil.

The particles that make up a given quantity of soil determine how well plants will fare there.

▲ Plants are the result of soil. Both their quality and quantity are dependent upon the quality of the soil in which they grow.

There are three primary types of soil: Sandy, or light; clay, or heavy; and loamy, or medium, the best of both.

Sandy soil is made up of relatively large, round particles with many open passageways. You can feel its gritty texture when you rub it between your fingers.

The many openings allow plenty of space for root development and easy flow of air, but they also permit easy flow of water. Sandy soil drains very quickly, without holding moisture or nutrients for very long.

By contrast, clay soil is made up of relatively small, flat particles with very little space between

▲ **The single most important thing that every gardener can do that will have the greatest impact on his or her harvest is to improve the soil in the garden.**

Soil Testing

A quick test for which type of soil your garden has to offer can be as simple as making a fist. Scoop a handful of your garden's soil into your palm and close your fist about it. If the soil crumbles and falls through your fingers, it tends towards the sandy extreme. If the soil forms a tight ball that doesn't fall apart easily, even when you open your fist, it tends towards the clay end of the spectrum. If the soil forms a ball, but then falls apart when you open your fist and prod it with a finger, it is near the happy medium of loamy soil.

Soil Quality

A critical aspect of your garden soil is where it falls on the sandy-clay scale. The optimum quality falls somewhere between the two extremes, in what we call loamy soil, a combination of the best qualities of the two extremes.

them. When wet it feels sticky and slick, like clay.

Roots, air and water all have relatively greater difficulty in penetrating its structure. Clay soil drains very slowly, holding moisture – often too much – and nutrients for long periods. However, when it does dry out, it grows rock-hard.

Loamy soil offers the best characteristics of both the extremes. It offers plenty of openings for roots, air and water, but drains slowly enough for plant roots to absorb water and nutrients.

And, of course, there are soil types that fall between all three of the primary classifications. Entire charts have been developed, but I've never found it of any additional use to know that a soil is clay-loamy or sandy-loamy.

Body-building for soil

The overriding consideration is that it isn't loamy and therefore needs improvement. Any soil can eventually be brought to the Nirvana-state of loamy with the addition of humus, which is also known as organic matter.

Humus is the decayed bodies of plants and animals. Picture it as millions of microscopic sponges. Added to sandy soil, humus increases the soil's capacity to hold water and nutrients. Added to clay soil, it provides more of the much needed openings. Loamy soils do not have the same dire need for this organic matter, but its addition will be nothing but beneficial.

In addition, humus is loaded with the living micro-organisms that are essential to healthy soil. In general, fertile soil contains no less than 5 per cent organic matter.

A quick stroll through the nearest wood or overgrown wasteland of tangles and weeds will attest to the importance of humus in the soil. Mother Nature uses none of the myriad fertilizers that we humans apply to our gardens and lawns in the name of bettering our growing conditions. Yet that wood or overgrown wasteland shoots out a dense, lush growth each and every year.

Naturally provided humus is the key here. With humus and no extra fertilizers, plants will grow quite nicely. However, the same cannot be said about fertilizers without humus. With a humus-packed soil, any fertilizer can be used much more fully by the plants.

Being organic, humus breaks down and decomposes quite quickly. Even most conventional, row-type gardeners add organic matter to their soil when they turn it each spring. That's good as far as it goes. But with intensive gardening, you will want to add humus every time you prepare to plant a new crop. On some spots in your garden, this could be three, four or five times a year.

▼ A well-maintained garden compost pile is the easiest, least expensive method for providing your own steady supply of humus. Although the pile does not need to be enclosed to function properly, many enclosures are available commercially for a better overall appearance.

Compost your way to success

To maintain such a supply of humus, you will want to have your own compost pile. A wide array of enclosures are available commercially for this purpose, ranging from wooden frames to recycled plastics to mesh wire walls. Even a large rubbish bin, with holes drilled in the bottom, or homemade frames of wood or cinder block can serve our purpose here. The important criterion is that the enclosure be at least 2–3 ft (60–90 cm) wide and deep. Larger enclosures will, of course, provide a greater supply of humus.

Into the enclosure, place 6–8 in (15–20 cm) of coarse organic material, such as weeds, leaves, grass clippings, hay and non-dairy/non-meat household waste. Many composters grind their organic household waste in blenders before adding it to the compost pile.

Onto this first layer of organic material, add a covering of "activator", such as bone meal or lime, or a starter compost. This should just cover the organic material. It does not need to be piled nearly as deep as the organic material. Then build your second layer of organic material, your second layer of "activator", your third layer of organic material, your third layer of "activator". And so on, until you've nearly filled your enclosure. Moisten each layer, but do not soak it. It should feel like a wrung-out sponge. Also, the pile must

▲ The basics for building better soil, clockwise from 12 o'clock, are aged cow manure, vermiculite, fine sand, peat moss, lime, compost and granular sulfate.

▼ Some home-mix fertilizer ingredients, from left, wood ashes, compost, blood meal and bone meal.

COMPOST

Each layer of coarse organic materials should be composed of lawn waste (weeds, leaves, grass clippings and the like) and organic, non-dairy/non-meat, household waste. Each activator layer should contain materials such as bone meal and lime, or a starter compost.

Water
Activator layer
Coarse organic material

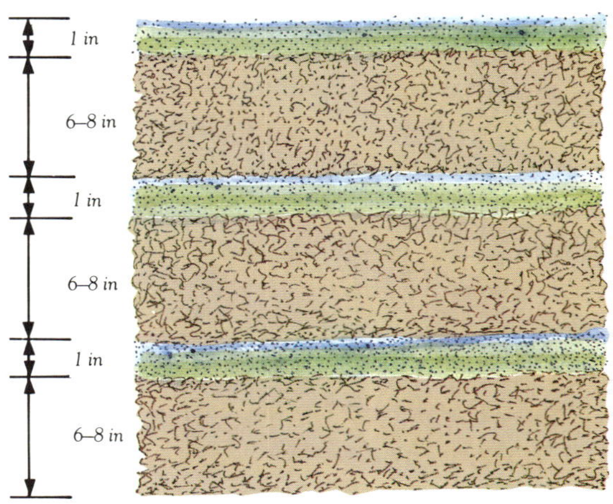

▲ **Local conditions often dictate the most available, free or low cost garden enhancers. If you have access to the coast, seaweed is a good source of nutrients.**

have air coming into contact with the composting materials throughout the process.

After two to three weeks, turn the pile by moving the drier outside materials to the centre and the wetter centre materials to the outside. Turn a second time in another two to three weeks. In about three months you will have a pile of humus ready for use in your soil.

The process can continue for more than three months, if you continue to add new organic matter and "activator" layers as the old layers decompose and settle. Most gardeners seem to begin their composting for the next spring as they clean up their gardens and lawns each autumn.

Vermiculite, mica rock super-heated until it explodes into tiny popcorn-like particles, is another important soil builder. It's one of the most lightweight materials that you'll ever encounter and holds water better than almost anything else. Like humus, it will improve the quality of any type of soil.

Although you'll have to buy your vermiculite, once added to your soil it will be there for many years to come. Coarse grade is the very best for our purposes, although the material is more generally available in the fine and medium grades. A bit of shopping around will prove worth the effort.

Peat moss, sort of a cross between humus and vermiculite (at least for our purposes), is the remains of plants that have been decomposing since prehistoric times on the bottoms of swampy areas. It's not quite as good as vermiculite at holding moisture in the soil, but it is less expensive and often more available in the large quantities that we are considering here.

A fourth soil builder under certain circumstances is sand, although we've described sandy soil as an undesirable characteristic. When extremely clay soil – clayey to the point that even heavy doses of vermiculite don't seem to be turning the tide – is encountered, small quantities of sand are often the quickest means to a change in soil texture.

Every garden's soil should have the equivalent of about one-third of its top 12-in (30-cm) volume in the form of these soil builders – humus, vermiculite and peat moss – added each spring. (As we noted, sand is considered a soil builder only under very special circumstances.) For very poor soil, it is not unreasonable to add as much as 50 per cent soil builders. In both of these instances, about 25 per cent of the additives should be vermiculite.

Correct pH levels

Another soil quality that must be considered before fertilizer is the pH of the soil. Without the proper pH balance in the soil, the plants will be

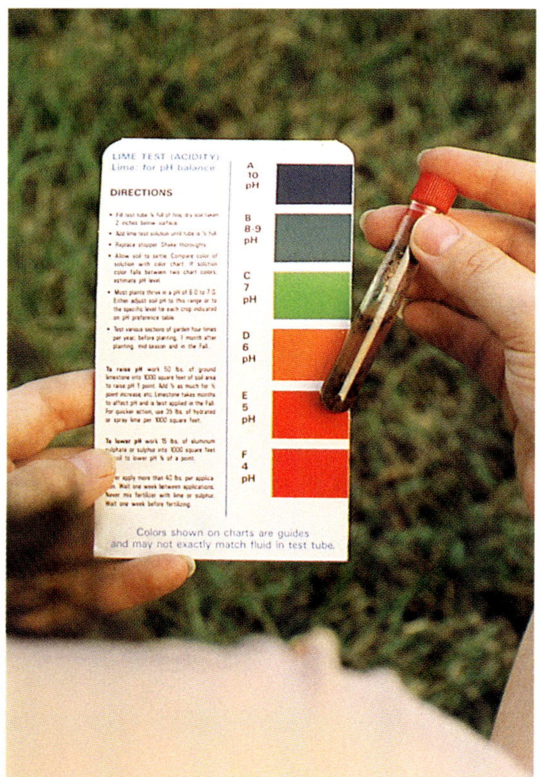

► **The do-it-yourself soil-pH test kits available at most garden centres and through most garden catalogues are generally accurate enough for use in the home garden.**

unable to make full use of any fertilizers that are added, much like the humus situation.

The pH scale reveals the acidity or alkalinity of a substance. The scale ranges from 0 (most acid) to 14 (most alkaline), with 7.0 representing the neutral status. Most plants fare quite well in the 6.0 to 7.0. (You can check the specific needs of individual vegetable types in the plant directory at the end of this book.)

Nearly every garden centre or catalogue offers a variety of easy-to-use, inexpensive, relatively accurate tests for checking the pH of your soil on your own. In addition, private soil laboratories (addresses from the Royal Horticultural Society) offer a battery of soil tests that include pH. Such an outside test can provide valuable information and I recommend it on a regular basis.

▲ **Plants don't care whether their nutrients come from organic or chemical sources. However, you should. This is one opportunity to control what goes into your food.**

You can raise and lower the pH of your soil by adding commonly available garden supplies. To raise the pH of light soil by 1 unit (ie. from 5.0 to 6.0), add 2½ oz (70 g) of hydrated lime, 3¼ oz (100 g) of dolomite or 4 oz (110 g) of ground limestone to 10 sq ft (3 sq m) of soil; for heavy soil, add 5½ oz (150 g) of hydrated lime, 8¾ oz (240 g) of dolomite or 9½ oz (275 g) of ground limestone to 10 sq ft (3 sq m).

To lower the pH of light soil by 1 unit (ie. from 8.0 to 7.0), add ¾ oz (20 g) of sulphur or 4¾ oz (130 g) of iron sulphate to 10 sq ft (3 sq m) of soil; for heavy soil, add 3¼ oz (90 g) of sulphur or 12 oz (340 g) of iron sulphate to 10 sq ft (3 sq m).

▲ **Plants need three major nutrients: nitrogen, phosphorus and potassium (potash). It's up to you to keep these supplied in sufficient quantities throughout the growing season.**

Fertilizers: Go organic

When the soil pH is balanced, the crops that you plant there will be able to draw their nourishment from the soil. Plants don't care if nutrients are supplied from organic sources or chemicals, but you should. Beyond the fact that one of the pleasures of gardening is some degree of control over what goes into your food, chemicals really add nothing of lasting value to your soil.

Yes, chemicals will nourish the plants, and they are readily available and easy to use. However, they can just as readily damage the soil, kill earthworms and beneficial micro-organisms that you want to live there, and damage plant roots.

Organic fertilizers, on the other hand, would

have to be used in nearly impossible quantities to do the same level of damage. Admittedly, they are sometimes more difficult to come by and generally more expensive. Neither of these conditions need to be obstacles any longer for you.

Plants need three major nutrients: Nitrogen for lush green growth; phosphorus for strong stem and seed development; and potash (Potassium) for strong root development and fruit production. They also need many minor trace elements, which will be supplied naturally if you regularly enhance your soil with humus as explained earlier.

It is relatively easy for you to mix your own nitrogen-phosphorus-potash fertilizer, using any of the following materials to achieve the correct formulation. Opinions vary widely over exactly what that formulation is, but one of the top-selling water-soluble plant foods on the market today uses a mix of 15–30–15. That translates to 15 parts nitrogen to 30 parts phosphorus to 15 parts potash, where the numbers can represent teaspoonfuls, bucketfuls, lbs or any other units of measurement.

The following materials, listed in the chart below, are just some of the most readily available that should be mixed in appropriate amounts to reach the 15–30–15 levels. The numbers represent the percentage of nitrogen, phosphorus and potash that the material contains.

It is often recommended that fertilizer should be applied by carefully working it into the top several inches of your soil to hold it close to your plants. But, during the growing season, this procedure can do serious damage to plant roots.

A less destructive method is to plant every plant in your garden with a band around it on the soil. The band should begin as a short lip of soil at the plant stem or the point where the seed is planted, dip into a shallow depression a few inches wide and end in a second, somewhat tall lip of soil. Fertilizer placed into the depression will be held in place, in close proximity to the plant, until it is dissolved into the soil.

This band method of planting will also hold water close to the plant and is a principal means for reducing water use in the garden.

▲ **Ignore any advice that would have you work the soil immediately adjacent to your plants to apply fertilizer. This will risk severe root damage.**

MATERIAL	NITROGEN %	PHOSPHORUS %	POTASH %
BLOOD MEAL	12.0	<1	<1
BONE MEAL	4.0	20.0	<1
CATTLE MANURE, DRIED	2.0	2.0	2.5
COFFEE GROUNDS	2.0	<1	<1
DRIED BLOOD	15.0	3.0	<1
FISH MEAL	7.5	10.0	2.0
LEAF MOLD, COMPOST	<1	<1	<1
ROCK PHOSPHATE	<1	40.0	4.5
ROCK POTASH	0	0	10.0
SEAWEED (DRIED, GROUND)	3.0	<1	5.0
SOYBEAN MEAL	6.0	1.2	1.5
WOOD ASHES	0	1.5	7.0

► **Rich, loamy soil like this is the best possible growing medium for garden crops.**

▲ Planting each of our crop plants in a slight depression, or with a moat-like band around it, will make the application of both fertilizer and water a much easier chore.

Mulch

After you have added all your soil builders, corrected pH levels and spread a general fertilizer, your garden should be covered by a layer of mulch. Anything from leaf mould to straw to sheets of plastic will function just fine as mulch, maintaining the moisture, temperature and friability of the soil.

Apply several inches of any organic material or one layer of 2– to 4–mil plastic after you have completed all of the above preparations on the soil. With organic materials you will want to use something that is easily moved, because you will simply push some aside to do your planting when the appropriate time arrives. With plastic, use clear rather than black. The old theory that black plastic heated the soil better than clear has been disproven. Black plastic heats itself more than the soil.

If you've had to work your soil in spring, plastic is the better mulching choice. While plastic will help to raise soil temperatures to planting levels, organic mulch can help to hold the colder temperatures of winter in the soil later into the year.

▼ Mulch creates a special layer across your garden that helps to seal in warmth and moisture while protecting plants that happen to lie on the ground.

Soil-building in progress

Everytime you harvest a crop from a particular spot in the garden you should also take an extra minute to refurbish the soil for your next crop. Add an appropriate amount of fertilizer in a thin, even layer over the space, material to correct the pH if necessary and a few inches of humus. Then turn the soil, thoroughly mixing all elements.

If the soil quality still is not as top-notch as you want, this is also a good opportunity to add more soil-builders, such as vermiculite or peat moss.

Following this procedure religiously, taking just an extra minute or two each time you harvest a crop, is all the soil work you will ever have to do again in the garden.

Autumn: Getting ready for next spring

In autumn, at the end of the normal gardening season, your soil will be relatively dry, soft and easy to work. Although your thoughts may be drifting away from gardening to more autumnal pursuits, a few hours spent on your garden now will pay big dividends next year.

True, many gardeners do leave the initial work with their soil for next spring. But, spring is not an optimum time of the year for this. The soil in spring is wet, hard and difficult to work. In addition, if it's too wet, working will only serve to compact and damage it.

Above all this, preparing your soil now will extend your growing season two to four weeks earlier next year. In those spaces where you

▲ **Mulch comes in many different forms, ranging from plastic sheets, leaves, to straw and grass clippings.**

won't be attempting to grow very late season crops, follow this procedure:

As soon as your summer crops have finished producing – generally when the first few frosts of autumn have killed them – remove all plant material from the garden. Those plants that show evidence of disease or insect damage should be completely removed from the area. The "clean" plants may be added to the compost pile.

Now, take another careful look at your soil. Once again check the texture and pH and add soil-builders or pH-correctors as needed.

Add 4–6 in (10–15 cm) of humus, a layer of dried cow manure and a fertilizer strong in phosphorus and potash. Turn the soil to a depth of about 12 in (8 cm), mixing all elements thoroughly.

Finally, cover the garden with at least 3 in (8 cm) of thick mulch. Pine boughs, non-composted leaves and hay are all good choices.

In place of the mulch you might want to plant a cover crop, such as winter rye grass, which many authors have referred to as a living mulch. Available as seed from most garden centres the rye grass will give you a lush, green cover through much of the winter. And next spring, when it's time to turn it over for planting, it will be at its lushest potential. Such a cover crop provides a nitrogen-rich organic boost to the soil in the spring.

▲ **A healthy earthworm community in your garden will help in the constant enhancement of the soil through the worms' clod-busting tunnelling and their freeing-up of nutrients in the soil for use by your plants.**

► **Even with vertical growing conditions and a healthy mulch layer, some crops will always need special attention. Such is the case with this 20-ounce plus tomato being protected from potential rot because of soil contact.**

Earthworms: Nature's soil-builders

One final, but essential component of the soil is the earthworm community. Most gardeners are pleased to see the creatures in their soil when they work it, taking them to be some sort of sign of healthy soil.

That view is correct, as far as it goes. Earthworms, everything from nightcrawlers to redworms, act as never-ending composters of the soil. They eat any organic matter and convert it to raw nutrients, readily available to plant roots, in their castings. They continuously break up the soil, building new passageways for air, water and plant roots, with their constant tunnelling.

After you have your soil ready for planting in the spring, you might want to consider buying several dozen worms and stocking them into the garden. They are available and cheap at bait shops, and even convenience stores, across the country.

WATER, THE ELIXIR OF LIFE

MORE DISAPPOINTMENTS IN gardening have been brought on by improper water conditions than by any other single cause, and often without the gardener ever knowing what exactly had happened. A basic understanding of soil–water–air–plant interactions is the best defence against water problems.

As we've noted in the previous chapter, different types of soil permit water penetration and retention at markedly different rates. However, since you're adding plenty of humus to your soil this need no longer be a concern.

We've also noted that compaction of the soil, caused by walking or driving over it repeatedly, will greatly reduce the soil's ability to absorb and hold water. But, you're now working with garden plots that you can reach without walking on them.

In addition, you're now maintaining a healthy depth of mulch over the top of all available garden spaces, right up to the bottom of the plant stems of your crops.

In other words, your soil is ready to receive the water and pass it, and the dissolved nutrients, along to the plants. However, there are some environmental factors over which you can exercise only limited control, such as wind. At various times during every growing season your garden will experience a period of windier than normal conditions. Plant leaves and the upper levels of the soil will dry out much faster than normal at these times. The same will happen during drought periods, which seem to have been on the increase during the past few years.

Your best defence against such environmental conditions is a thorough understanding of the mechanism involved in getting water to your plants.

As water enters the soil, whether from natural rainfall or your watering, it moves down through

▲ **Improper watering is probably the cause of more setbacks in the garden than any one single source, after poor soil conditions, and often without the gardener knowing they exist.**

the passageways that we've already discussed, pushing the air that was in the passageways out ahead of it. As the water continues its downward march, air from the surface follows in its path and refills the passageways.

Although we don't normally think of it, plant roots need air just as much as they need water. Air movement through the passageways takes the carbon dioxide given off by the roots and delivers a supply of fresh oxygen.

If water fills the passageways for too long a period at any one time – an undesirable condition we often hear referred to as waterlogged or poor drainage – the oxygen supply to the roots is cut off. When this condition exists, the plant stops growing. On the other hand, when the plant goes too long without enough water – another undesirable condition, known as water stress – it again stops growing.

Whenever the plant receives the signal to stop growing, for whatever reason, its internal mechanisms are led to "believe" that the plant is dying. Now, before death can take over, the plant puts everything it has into reproduction. Blossom and seed production become its sole focus. The internal chemistry of the plant changes as part of this process, leading to significant and undesir-

► **Constant and adequate supplies of water are absolutely necessary for quality and quantity production of most crops, particularly the fruit and seed crops such as tomatoes.**

able changes in the taste of any fruits it already bears or that it now produces.

If conditions return to normal, growth will begin again in its normal manner. But the plant has been stressed and the ultimate harvest from that plant has been affected. Repeated stressing throughout the growth of a plant will lead to a very low-quality harvest.

Too much water can also lead to inappropriate growth in some crops, particularly the fruit and seed crops. Beans, sweetcorn, cucumbers, mel ons, peppers, marrow and tomatoes all will send out bushy growths of leaves – at the expense of their fruits and seeds – under these conditions.

Another factor that is generally not visible at the surface of the soil is the dispersion of water as it soaks down through the passageways in the soil. It spreads out substantially as it moves downwards. On the surface, it might appear to cover a foot or so. But just a foot down, it might already have spread over an area of more than 2 ft (61 cm). Down another foot, it might be spread to more than 4 ft (122 cm).

As you can now see, no book on the subject can tell you exactly when to water and how much water to apply. As a general guideline, ideal watering conditions will deliver one inch of water to the garden every week during the gardening season. This translates into a bit more than a half-gallon of water for every square foot of growing space every week.

It's better for that water to be supplied in just a few soaking sessions each week, rather than in small spurts every day or every other day. The former method gets the water down deep and encourages strong, deep root growth. The latter supplies water only to the two few inches of the soil and forces the plants to send out shallow root systems to make use of that surface moisture.

With the band method of planting that we detailed in our chapter on understanding your soil, the inch-deep "moat" around every plant fulfils this function very nicely. As the "moat" is filled, it holds water in close proximity to the plant's roots long enough for the water to soak slowly and deeply into the soil.

Another way to accomplish this slow delivery of water is to sink a can, inverted plastic milk or water jug, or some similar container a few inches into the soil next to each plant. The container should be placed there when the plant is planted to avoid any potential damage to the plant's roots. Drill or punch a dozen or two tiny holes into the bottom of the can, or a few larger holes into the cap of the inverted plastic jug, before positioning it in the soil.

Using such reservoirs allows you to dole out more precisely exact quantities of water to your plants. Combine them with a backyard rain gauge and the most reliable weather forecast you've been able to find for your area, and you're ready to supply optimum water conditions. After each bit of natural rainfall check the rain gauge and jot down the reading on a slip of paper, where you're recording all water delivered to the garden for the week.

Suppose that the rain gauge tells you that a storm on Sunday dropped a ¼ in (30 mm) of water, it's now Wednesday and no additional rainfall is expected for the rest of the week. You might want to supply a quart or a quart-and-a-half of water in each reservoir, which combined with the ¼ in (30 mm) of rainfall – equivalent to another quart or so – will supply more than half of the water that the plant needs for that week.

Of course, you must temper all such quantity

recommendations with your exact conditions. If it takes a few hours for water that you've supplied in a reservoir to soak away into the soil, you're probably pretty close to the mark. On the other hand, if it takes four or five hours for this to happen, something isn't working correctly and you should recheck everything we've discussed relating to soil and water conditions.

You will also want to temper your water decisions with your own observations. Stick your finger into the soil. Does it feel moist or dry? Do your plants look wilted after a dry, hot, sunny day, but recover during the evening? Or do they look wilted first thing in the morning?

The most widely used method of watering is with the garden hose. This also happens to be the most ineffective and potentially harmful method. It is ineffective because so much of the water lands in places that really are not involved in growing plants. It is potentially harmful because users of this method generally do not have the time that would really be needed to deliver a good, deep-soaking supply of water through this method and because it wets the leaves and stems of the plants, increasing their susceptibility to diseases.

The reservoir methods that we outlined earlier avoid these problems by delivering the quantity of water needed over a long enough period for deep-soaking and by delivering that water at ground level. A substantial, added benefit of reservoir watering arises from the precision involved. Water is delivered only to the crop plants and not to other areas, where weeds would be likely to grow. Without water, those weeds will have a very tough time of it taking hold.

▲ Plastic sheets spread over the garden help to conserve ground moisture. They also help to heat the soil in the spring and protect it from hard, driving rains in the cold season.

Another method of slow, soaking water delivery is the seep, dripper, trickler or bubbler hose. This is a basic hose that has many miniscule holes drilled along its entire length or that has been constructed on porous material. When water is run through the hose, it slowly drips, trickles or seeps through the tiny holes and openings. The hose is left "running" for a few hours at a time to provide the deep-soaking that we need. The seep hose that I use around my plants delivers about 1 gall (5 l) per minute along its entire 50-feet length at a water pressure of 5 lbs (2 kg) per square inch and about 3½ gall (15 l) per minute at 30 lbs (12 kg) per square inch.

Water supplied to your reservoirs should be warm, about room temperature. You can achieve this in several ways:

- A large rain barrel or two, set up at the bottom of the drainpipes of your home's roof-drainage system generally will maintain an adequate supply of sun-warmed water throughout much of the gardening season. Of course, some sort of covering will be needed for each barrel to keep water-breeding insects, such as mosquitoes, from making their homes there.
- Several buckets, as many as it seems to require to hold enough water for your garden's needs, can be filled from the spigot or from the

◀ A seep, trickling or bubbling hose will provide a regulated amount of water over an extended period, allowing for the healthy soaking type of watering that most garden crops need at maturity.

hose and allowed to warm in the sun before use. This method is recommended by many authors because it also allows for chemicals, such as chlorine, added by the local water company to evaporate off, if the water sits for 24 hours.

If such chemicals in the water are of concern to you, and they probably should be, you might consider adding an inexpensive filter to your outdoor water tap, just as you would to the tap over the kitchen sink.

- Alternately, your garden hose can be left coiled in full sunlight for a few hours before being used for watering.

To confuse the matter further, different plants have different water needs. The directory at the end of this book describes water requirements for each crop as either heavy, medium or low. Those plants that have heavy requirements generally need about 1 gall (5 l) per square foot each week; medium, about ¾ gall (3 l) per square foot each week; and low, about ½ gall (2 l) per square foot each week.

Freshly planted seeds and transplants need a steady supply of water in the first inch or two of the soil surface. The seed needs the moisture to germinate and sprout. The transplant needs the moisture to help it through the period of stress that nearly always accompanies being transplanted. At these times, if the top few inches of soil dry out the plant probably will be lost.

As young plants grow upward, their roots grow downward. As a result, the depth to which water must be supplied increases as well.

▼ Water reservoirs, such as this commercially available plant waterer, are another good method for allowing water to soak slowly into the ground. They will also help to hold the weeds at bay.

Dealing with a Poor-Drainage Area

Whenever possible, avoid poor drainage areas – those spots where water stands on the surface of the soil for several hours after a rainfall – in your garden.

These areas can also occur below the surface. If you suspect this condition exists in your garden, dig a few foot-wide/foot-deep holes in the area under question and wait for the next rain storm. After the storm, check the water in the hole periodically to see how long it takes to drain away. Three to four hours is the maximum that any spot should require for drainage, if you want to use it successfully as part of your garden.

The simplest method of dealing with basic drainage problems is the addition of large amounts of humus to the soil, as we've already outlined in our chapter on soil. In slightly more severe instances the addition of some sand might be needed.

But for the most severe cases – if you're absolutely dead-set on using that spot in your garden – you will need to turn your attention to the layer of soil beneath the top 18–24 in (46–60 cm) that form the basis for most of your plant roots. Every 3 or 4 ft (90–122 cm) across the poor drainage area, dig a 2-ft (61-cm) deep ditch that slants towards the nearest spot of lower elevation. Into the bottom 6–8 in (15–20 cm) of the ditch, place a mixture of two parts gravel and one part sand. Return the original soil, enhanced with humus, into the remainder of the ditch. Are you sure you can't just avoid the spot?

STARTING EARLIER, ENDING LATER

Throughout most of the British Isles the gardening season runs from early May to mid- or late-September, for the conventional gardeners. They must pack all their planting and growing into about five months, total.

But for those of you ready to move on to new ways of thinking about gardening, a hefty arsenal of special techniques awaits your command to advance the frontiers of the gardening season, both earlier in spring and later in autumn. The price for moving outside the normal parameters of the growing season is additional work and a much greater chance for disappointment.

Simplest among these techniques is just to go ahead and plant some of the cool-weather crops that the seed packets tell you can be planted outside before the last spring frost even earlier than suggested on the packets. In all but the northernmost UK, it's entirely possible to sneak an entire extra crop of plants such as kale, lettuce, radishes, spinach and Swiss chard into your growing plan by the time the suggested planting date rolls around. Of course, you must be aware that there's a fifty-fifty chance of losing the crop to unexpected bouts of cold and frost.

This same feat can be accomplished again at the end of the normal autumn planting period. Most gardeners do not even take advantage of the benefits of one autumn planting, which can include all of the above crops, as well as broad beans, broccoli, Brussels sprouts, cabbage, cauliflower, endive, kohlrabi, onions and peas. So if you also plant the second autumn crop of kale, lettuce, radishes, spinach and Swiss chard, you've actually gained an additional two crops at the end of the normal growing season.

The first autumn crop should be started as specified for individual plants in the directory at the end of this book. The second should be started a few weeks later to provide staggered harvests until the first really hard frost of autumn. Many of the crops described here as appropriate for this second autumn crop will withstand the first few lighter frosts with little or no real damage.

▼ The normal early May to September gardening season can be greatly extended with the many new techniques outlined in this book.

In the very early spring and late autumn, the leaf and head crops can get a boost through the use of a portable cold frame that you can easily make at home. The only tools you will need are a saw, hammer, wood drill with a ¼–in (6 mm) bit, screwdriver and paintbrush.

THE MATERIALS YOU WILL NEED ARE:

- Three 12-ft (3.65 m)-long 2×6s (framing timber type).
- One board (any wood type), 150 in (381 cm) long, 2½–3 in (6–8 cm) and 1 in (2½ cm) thick.
- One sheet of 3-mil, clear plastic, 45–50 in (114–727 cm).
- 36 10-penny nails.
- Four straight metal reinforcement bands with screw holes, ¾ in (2 cm) wide, ⅛–¼ in (6 mm) thick.
- Eight ¾ in (2 cm) screws, appropriate to the size of the screw holes in the metal reinforcement bands.
- A dozen or so drawing pins.
- Wood glue.
- Small bit of black paint.

You are going to build three frames from the 2×6s and a framed, plastic lid from the smaller board and plastic sheet.

Begin by cutting the first 2×6 into four pieces: two of 45 in (114 cm) in length and two of 24 in (61 cm) in length. Depending upon how your timber supplier cuts the 2×6s, you will have anything up to an extra 6 in (15 cm) of board left over after all your cuts have been made. This is a waste but it makes very good kindling.

Nail the four pieces together, with two 3-in (7.5-cm) nails at each corner, into a frame that measures 24 in (61 cm) wide and 48–49 in (122 cm) long (depending upon the exact width of your 2×6s). The frame should have the same 6-in (15 cm) dimension of your timber as its depth.

Repeat this procedure with each of your three 2×6s, until you have built three frames of exactly the same dimensions.

Place one of your frames on a flat area and, on the two 24-in (61-cm) sides splotch a ¼-in (6 mm) blot of black paint about 4 in (10 cm) from each corner and dead-centre on the 2-in (5-cm) top of the board. Before the paint dries, position a second frame on top of the first. Repeat with the third frame on top of the second.

Remove the two top frames and drill ¼-inch holes (about 2 in (5 cm) deep) at each of the paint marks on the top of the bottom frame. Do the same at the paint marks on the top and bottom of the second frame, and the same at the paint marks on the bottom of the top frame.

When you want to stack your three frames into one, taller frame, simply slip a 3-in (7.5-cm) nail into each of the top holes on the bottom frame and ease the holes of the middle frame's bottom over the tops of the nails. Do the same thing to attach the top frame to the middle.

Paint the inside of each frame white.

Now, cut the smaller board into four pieces that will exactly match the outside dimensions of your frames and a fifth piece that extends across the middle of their width. Join them with the metal reinforcement bands and screws, with wood glue between the joints. Attach the middle crosspiece with wood glue. Wrap the plastic sheet around the outside of the frame and attach it securely in place with the drawing pins. This is the lid for your frames.

(Note • You don't necessarily need to start off with the lengths of boards described here. You can use any lengths of board that will give you the dimensions described here, or other dimensions of your own design.)

There are several ways to put your frames into use. Place a single-level frame with the lid on it over a patch of garden even before the last snow has fallen. Dig its sides down into the soil a few inches, with a noticeable slant of the sides so that the lid leans to the south. When the soil beneath the frame has dried to the point that it can pass the fist-test for workable soil described in chapter four, you can plant your first crop of leaf vegetables and radishes. In general, this will be many weeks before you would ever consider planting anything outside under any other conditions. As a matter of fact, this technique usually will produce harvestable salad crops about the time that you are ready to plant what would normally be your earliest crop outside.

A second frame, with a second lid that you will need to build, can be placed over another

◀ The components of a fully functional portable cold frame are three 2×6 frames, a framed plastic lid and a dozen 3-in (7.5 cm) nails.

▶ Dig the bottom frame into the soil at a strong angle slanting towards the south. This maximizes exposure to direct sunlight.

◀ A single-level frame with lid can be used for both early and late crops of cool-weather plants, such as lettuce, spinach and radishes. The frame provides extra warming of the soil and protection from the elements.

▶ Heavy nails placed loosely in pre-drilled holes provide a simple joining mechanism for linking the different frames into taller structures. If you have the necessary tools, you will want to grind the heads from the nails.

◀ It's easy to accommodate extra growth by adding a second level. Leaving the lid off can provide protection from winds and shelter from the sun for transplants being hardened off for outdoor living.

▶ With a third level nearly all gardening conditions can be accommodated. Add the plastic lid and you might be able to raise transplants to fully grown plants in the same spot.

section of the garden about four weeks before the normal early season planting dates. This will dry the soil to the workable point and warm it for planting over the next four weeks.

The third frame, again with another lid that you will need to build, can be placed elsewhere in the garden to serve as a hot-house to start germinating your seedlings for later transplanting about the garden.

In the autumn the three frames can be stacked up on top of each other, with the bottom one nearly buried in the soil, and slanted towards the south. Mix a soil-builder-rich soil into the area inside the box and plant various areas with whatever you want among the crops described for late planting earlier in this chapter.

As it is, this box will support a healthy harvest into very late autumn. As winter approaches the lid should be added and an insulating material, such as bales of hay, should be stacked along the outsides. With luck, you'll be picking salad greens from the box well into winter.

The portable cold frames can also give you much earlier starting with your warm-season crops. About four weeks before you would normally plant those crops as seeds indoors, place a single-level frame with lid over the spot where you want to raise the crops. About two weeks later, still two weeks before your normal starting time, plant your seeds directly on location. These plants generally will grow as though they were indoors or in a greenhouse, but they will never have to undergo the stress of transplanting. As a result they will be hardier, faster growing and quicker to blossom and set fruit.

During the hot, summer months a portable cold frame or two stacked on top of one another can provide a sheltered environment to raise an extra crop of cold-season crops, such as greens and radishes, in mid-summer. Replace the plastic lid with a screen lid to allow some filtered sunlight to reach the crops. Try to use varieties of these crops that are described as "heat resistant" or "slow to bolt" for this special use.

At times, while using the portable cold frame, you will need to provide some venting to prevent too great a build-up of heat and humidity. At these times it's a simple matter just to slide the plastic lid down a bit along the top of the top frame. The further you slide the lid, the more ventilation you will gain.

With your frames slanted to the south, the hot air and humidity will naturally flow towards the highest point within the cold frame. That will be the spot where you are providing the opening as you slide the lid downward. But, cold air from the outside won't move into and around the cold frame as quickly.

A simpler, easier-to-build device can be made to perform many of the same tasks as the portable cold frame. Bending fence wire, with 2×2 to 4×4 openings, into a half-circle with a highest point near the centre of the bend about 10 or 12 in (25–30 cm) above the ground when the two ends are resting on the ground. The length of this frame can be whatever length works best in your garden situation. This structure can be used for all of the following uses.

- Without any additions, the frame can be placed over seedlings such as beans and sweetcorn that are susceptible to attack from birds and animals. It will hold those creatures away from the tender young plants until they grow large enough to be safe from attack.
- The frame can be used in this same unadorned manner to support low-growing bush crops, such as beans. The seeds can be planted directly under the frame and the plants can then be allowed to grow right through the openings.
- Place 3-mil, clear plastic over the frame and it can be used to speed the drying and heating of the soil in the spring, as we have already described for the portable cold frame. Attach the plastic to the frame with clothespegs.
- Substitute screening, cheesecloth or some other material that partially filters the sunlight and the frame will provide the needed shade for growing crops like lettuce and radish, which are normally cool-season crops, throughout the summer. Remember to better your chances in this endeavour by using varieties of the plants that are "slow to bolt" or "heat resistant".

This same arrangement should be used to provide shade and wind-protection for all new transplants being moved outdoors.

- As the date of the first autumn frost approaches, any vertically grown crops that are still producing or ripening fruits can be carefully

▲ **Apply plastic sheets over the garden several weeks before you plan to work the soil. This generally will get the soil ready for working earlier than normal in the spring.**

unattached from their supports and gently laid into a 6-in (15-cm)-deep trench dug at their base and lined with a layer of straw. A plastic-covered tunnel-frame placed over the top of the plant and trench will extend the productive life of the plant beyond that first frost.

Clear plastic sheets can be applied directly over the garden, without any frames, several weeks before your plan to work the soil. As explained earlier in this chapter for other devices, the sheets will also dry and heat the soil much earlier than would occur if the soil was left to natural processes.

Transplants: Jump-start on growth

Transplants have been the conventional gardener's primary head-start mechanism for many years. The same seeds that generate transplants can be planted directly into their assigned locations in the garden, but only with an accompanying loss of many weeks of growth that could already be behind them had they been started indoors, in a greenhouse or in a portable cold frame that is heated.

Not only do transplants buy extra growing time for the gardener, they also save space in the garden, particularly in the intensive-style garden we've been discussing throughout this book. By starting as many plants under transplant conditions, either completely removed from the garden or in a small corner of the garden, you won't be using the space in most of the garden as a nursery for young plants. Your garden space can be used exclusively for the final stages of plant growth, when the plants are reaching their full mature size, blossoming and setting fruit. This is a long-distance extension of the succession planting plans that we discussed in chapter three.

(NOTE • We recommend starting your own transplants from seed at home rather than buying seedlings from a local nursery or garden centre. You will find you have a much greater variety of

► **Transplants are one conventional method for jump-starting many plants. They provide a gain of several weeks over planting seeds directly into the garden. While they not only buy extra growing time, they also save space in the garden. While they are reaching the point that they can be planted in the garden, other crops can be using the same space.**

transplants to choose from and you can completely control every aspect of the transplants life from germination to garden. There's also the issue of cost. Seeds are much less expensive than seedlings.)

Any seeds that are large enough to permit the procedure will benefit from a pre-soaking prior to planting. This can be done either in a seed tray or pot or directly in the garden. Soak them in lukewarm water overnight, making sure that they don't have the chance to dry out once they've been wetted.

In this way you can give the seeds a significant boost that can have repercussions for the rest of their lives. In effect you are compressing the period over which the seeds must soak up the necessary water to germinate and sprout. Any time you can give your plants such a hand-up will enhance their growth and food production. The period from seed to sprout is particularly crucial.

The one drawback with transplants – and it's a big one – is the shock that every seedling goes through every time it's transplanted. Although the shock can range from very slight to very severe, it is unavoidable and will temporarily slow or halt the plant's growth.

To limit the shock for your transplants, start them from seed in containers where they can continue to grow until the time comes to plant them directly into the spaces in the garden. Furthermore, use containers that can be sacrificed at garden-planting time.

The 1 lb (450 g) soft-margarine tubs that nearly every household seems to collect at phenomenal rates are fine containers for this, as are the various sized plastic containers used for take-away soup or drinks by many restaurants, as well as large family-sized yogurt containers. There are many other similar containers that can be recycled practically after their intended uses have been fulfilled.

Punch or drill a few dozen tiny holes into the bottom of the container. Fill it with a mixture of 70 per cent potting soil and 30 per cent vermiculite. Remove a central circle (1–1½ in (2.5–4 cm) diameter) from the top 1½ in (4 cm) of the soil-vermiculite mix and replace half of that with pure vermiculite. Place your seed – remembering to put just one single seed in each container – on top of the vermiculite at the centre and fill in the rest of the hole with vermiculite.

Set the container in a pan of water for 30 minutes or so, long enough to allow the soil and vermiculite to become moist. For an extra boost, you might dissolve a small quantity of fish meal to the water. When vermiculite becomes saturated with water, it generally changes to a noticeable darker shade.

If the original lid for the container is clear plastic, you can use it as the covering for your new mini-hothouse. Drill a few tiny holes in it and put it in place on the container. If the original lid was not clear, stretch a piece of clingfilm over the top of the container, not forgetting to prick some holes in it.

▲ No matter how gently you handle your seedlings, every one of them will experience transplant stress to a greater or lesser extent. Be very careful and minimize handling as much as you can.

Keep the soil and vermiculite moist throughout the time that the seed and later the seedling occupies the container. When the seedling begins to show, remove the lid or clingfilm.

When the time comes to transplant the seedling into the garden – after hardening it off for a few days – use a long-pointed, very sharp pair of scissors to cut down through the sides of the container, through the bottom of the container and up through the opposite side. You're splitting the container into two halves to remove it from around the seedling, rather than forcing the seedling out of the container. Do this very carefully, with constant concern about not jogging the plant or pulling on its roots, and you will minimize transplant shock as much as you possibly can.

TRANSPLANT OR DIRECT-SEED

Some vegetables fare very poorly when transplanted – notably the root crops – even when the most careful techniques are used. These should also be direct-seeded in the garden. Others can be treated as transplant or direct-seed. And still others, fare much better when transplanted. This is indicated in the chart below.

CROP	DIRECT-SEED ONLY	TRANSPLANT OR DIRECT-SEED	TRANSPLANT
ASPARAGUS		X	
AUBERGINE			X
BEANS (BROAD)	X		
BEANS (RUNNER)	X		
BEANS (FRENCH)	X		
BEETROOT	X		
BROCCOLI			X
BRUSSELS SPROUTS			X
CABBAGE			X
CARROTS	X		
CAULIFLOWER			X
COURGETTES			X
CUCUMBERS		X	
ENDIVE		X	
GARLIC	X		
KALE		X	
KOHLRABI		X	
LEEKS		X	
LETTUCE		X	
MARROWS	X		
MELON		X	
ONIONS		X	
PARSLEY			X
PEAS	X		
PEPPERS			X
POTATO	X		
RADISHES	X		
SPINACH	X		
SWEETCORN	X		
SWEET POTATO			X
SWISS CHARD		X	
TOMATOES			X

(NOTE • Many sizes and descriptions of peat pots and peat pellets are sold for this same purpose. It is generally claimed that the plant roots will grow right through them and they will decompose in a short time when placed in the garden. However, many of us have found that plant roots cannot penetrate them, they do not easily disintegrate in the garden and can even act like a sponge to suck moisture away from the plant roots so it is best to avoid them.)

Seeds need no light for germination and sprouting. In most cases, absolute darkness is not a necessity either. When moisture and heat spark activity inside the seed, the first external action will be to send down primary roots. Only after those roots have secured themselves will the seed push out in an upwards direction.

As soon as the tiny plant breaks through the soil, light becomes a necessity. Many authors have recommended placing these plants on windowsills with southern exposures to grow them to transplant size. However, it is a very rare windowsill that receives an amount of sunlight adequate for this purpose.

Most transplants raised on windowsills will be tall and spindly. They generally will not have the same vigour of transplants grown in direct sunlight or under fluorescent lights. As a result, they will produce a much reduced crop.

Throughout this period, from seed to transplant, you will need to maintain a daily check-up routine for all of your containers and later for the young plants. The warm, moist conditions that are best for the tiny seedlings are also optimum growing conditions for really nasty things, like disease-causing bacteria.

The portable cold frame can be used as a mini-greenhouse. Use all three frames stacked on top of one another, with the bottom frame nearly buried in the soil and the plastic-covered lid attached. As usual, the frame should slant strongly toward the south. Outline the outside of the frame all around with bales of hay and lay a heating coil in the bottom.

Start your transplants in the frame at the same time and in the same manner that you would if you were raising them indoors. When working with the containers, soil and small plants, be careful not to expose them to cold outside temperatures for more than a few seconds at a time and on no account risk exposing them to cold, or even cool, winds.

(NOTE • Regardless of the exact location of your future transplants, temperatures should be maintained at a constant 70°–80°F (27°C) to encourage proper germination. For many types of vegetables, the time for germination will double with each 10–12 degree drop below 70°F (27°C).

◀ **Some gardeners have had success in starting their transplants in outdoor mini-greenhouses. Temperatures for proper germination must be maintained in the 70-80°F (27°C) range.**

When moving transplants outdoors you first want to take them through several days of "hardening off". They've been raised in a completely protected environment to this point and now you're about to expose them to the sun, wind and everything else that the real world can throw at them. You need to introduce them to this gradually, exposing them to the outdoors for just a few hours the first day and completely protecting them from direct sunlight. With each new day, expose them for a few more hours, but continue to protect them against any direct sunlight.

◀ Transplants have been raised in a totally protected environment. They require several days of gradual "hardening off" when being moved into the outdoor garden environment.

After five or six days, they are ready to be moved into their permanent home in the garden. Continue to shade them from the sunlight for several more days, but gradually allow more and more sunlight to fall on them directly. After another four or five days, they are "hardened off". No additional protection from the elements will generally be needed.

Watch your tender young plants steadfastly during their first few days, checking on them at least daily. They are very susceptible to the vagaries of nature at this point. They and their soil must not be allowed to dry out. The sooner that you spot a problem, the less damage that will be done to the seedlings.

This adage holds true for all your garden crops, no matter how far along the growth cycle they might be. A couple of minutes spent checking all the plants daily will repay you big dividends in overall harvest.

The soil into which you place your transplants should be the very best that you have to offer. Your normal garden soil is now in tip-top shape, but you can enhance those spaces intended for transplants even further.

Mix equal parts of your already enhanced garden soil, vermiculite, humus, peat moss; ⅓ part of coarse sand; ½ part of wood ashes; and an appropriate amount of fertilizer for the size of the space you're working. Check the pH and balance it into the 6.0–8.0 zone.

The same vermiculite-based planting method that we outlined earlier for starting seeds for transplants can also be applied to those crops that are direct-seeded into the garden. Make a 1-in (2.5-cm)-diameter, ½-in (12-mm)-deep hole for each small seed, such as carrot, or a 1-in (2.5-cm)-diameter, ¾-in (18-mm)-deep hole for each larger seed, such as bean. Fill the hole halfway with vermiculite and drop your one seed – only one seed per hole – onto the centre of the vermiculite. Fill the hole the rest of the way with vermiculite. Spray the hole and its immediate vicinity with a fine mist of water until the vermiculite and soil is moist.

▼ The soil into which you place transplants should be the very best that you have to offer, enhanced even beyond the top quality you've already achieved in your general garden soil.

THE ONE-SEED/ONE-SPACE METHOD

Throughout this book you encounter admonitions to plant only one seed to each space in your garden. We encourage you to do this because a seed supplied by a reputable catalogue company generally will germinate and sprout and therefore the additional seeds are excess and needless baggage. But we also encourage this single-seed method because it saves you work when you don't have to go back and thin out the extra seedlings and it produces stronger seedlings that never need to compete for air, water and nutrients.

This may be a difficult method to force upon yourself. Human nature will make you wonder if most of the seeds you plant will actually produce. If this is too much of a concern for you to bear, go ahead and plant two or three seeds per space. But, be ready to go back and thin out the excess.

Because you'll be using far fewer seeds each gardening season under this single-seed method, you're going to have a coinciding increase in the number of leftover seeds each year. Our solution to this is to save seeds from one year to the next. To do this you must shield the seeds from the two elements that combine to produce germination: moisture and heat. Enclosing the seeds in a dry, sealed jar and then storing the jar in the back of the refrigerator accomplishes both of these objectives. You should maintain your seeds in this manner even during the active gardening season, taking them out just long enough to remove enough for immediate planting. Never plant directly from the seed packet. This exposes seeds to both moisture and heat at the same time.

Seeds kept under these optimum conditions will remain viable for surprisingly long periods: Asparagus, 3 years; aubergine, 4; beans, 3; beetroot, 4; broccoli, 3; Brussels sprouts, 4; cabbage, 4; carrots, 3; cauliflower, 4; sweetcorn, 2; cucumbers, 5; endive, 5; kale, curly-leaved, 4; kale, plain-leaved, 5; kohlrabi, 3; leeks, 2; lettuce, 6; marrow, 4; onions, 1; parsley, 1; peas, 3; peppers, 2; radishes, 5; spinach, 3; Swiss chard, 4; and tomatoes, 4.

Spread 10 seeds of the type that you want to test on a moist kitchen roll and roll the whole affair into a moist tea towel.

Place the rolled tea towel into a plastic bag and seal the bag with a metal wire closure. Leave the package in some location that receives even heat, such as the top of your refrigerator.

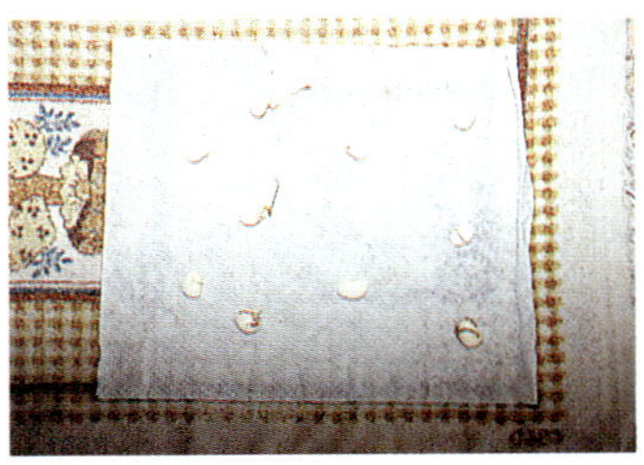

At the end of the correct germination period, multiply the number of seeds that have sprouted by 10. This gives you a general idea about how well the rest of the seeds in the batch will fare when planted.

Many gardeners find it difficult to believe that the seeds they buy can "be good" even the following year, let alone 4 or 5 years later, even under the best of storage conditions. For them there is the germination test:

- *Place 10 seeds of the same type (the type being tested) onto a kitchen roll and moisten the roll so that it's wet to the touch but not dripping.*
- *Roll the kitchen roll into a straw-like arrangement, rolling the seeds up as you proceed.*
- *Place the kitchen roll on a wet tea towel and roll the tea towel around it.*
- *Place the tea towel, with the kitchen roll and seeds rolled inside, into a plastic bag. The type that a loaf of bread comes in is fine.*
- *Mark the date and seed variety on the bag with a felt-tip marker. Seal the open end of the bag with a metal wire closure. Place it on top of the refrigerator or hot water tank.*
- *Referring to the seed packet for the date when the seeds should germinate and sprout, check on the seeds about halfway to that date. Re-moisten the kitchen roll if needed. Note the number of seeds that have already sprouted. Re-seal the bag and place it on top of your heat source.*
- *On the date provided by the seed packet, check the seeds.*
- *Multiply the number that have sprouted by 10. This gives you the percentage that sprouted, which can be applied with some certainty to all the seeds in that packet. Less than 50 per cent is cause for concern and reason to plant extras of these seeds in each garden space or seed tray or pot.*

WEEDS, INSECTS, DISEASES AND OTHER PESTS

If you’re now using the techniques we’ve discussed throughout this book, you’re already doing a great deal to cut down on weeds, insects and diseases in your garden.

As you spend a few minutes each day or every other day harvesting crops, watering your plants or otherwise tending to the minimal maintenance duties that are necessary, you are providing the first line of defence. Your contact with your plants is a great deal more intimate than it was under the old row-type methods of gardening. All of your plants are now no more than a couple of feet away from your nose. In addition, your vine crops are growing vertically, offering a much easier inspection than if they were sprawled across the ground.

In most instances, you’re going to notice any problem before it has a chance to really have much of an impact. You’ll be able to take corrective action before you have a full-blown infestation on your hands.

For many insects, that corrective action will entail the simple, physical removal of the offending creature and a quick squashing under the heel. The weekly spraying with offensive and environmentally dangerous chemicals is a thing of the past for you.

When you remove an insect from one of your plants, you should also expunge any evidence of the damage that it left behind. Chewed areas on leaves, spotted foliage and the like should be cut from the plant with a small pair of secateurs. Droppings, eggs and the like should be washed from the plant with a burst of water. In this way, you won’t mistake this old evidence of a pest long since removed for evidence that a new pest has set up housekeeping. Similarly, this will prevent new damage being cloaked behind old, familiar signs of damage.

◀ **Beneficial: Ladybird beetles are strong natural predators on many of garden pests. A particular target is the highly destructive aphid.**

A brief directory of some of the most common insect pests follows. If manual removal and disposal fails to resolve the problem, then try the additional treatments which are listed in order from the least severe to the most.

Insect pests

APHID soft, light green, egg-shaped bodies less than $\frac{1}{10}$ of an inch long. They produce honeydew that attracts ants. Spray the aphids with garlic or onion water. Introduce ladybird beetles and/or lacewings to the garden.

APPLE SAWFLY maggots up to $\frac{1}{2}$ in (1.3 cm) long of this tiny fly burrow into developing apples where they cause a scar on the surface of the apple. They are best controlled by picking and burning tunnelled fruitlets.

ASPARAGUS BEETLE shiny black wing covers with four white rectangles across back and red at edges, red thorax, $\frac{1}{4}$ in (6 mm) long. The larva is grey to green with a black head and legs, less than $\frac{1}{4}$ in (6 mm) long. Introduce ladybird beetles and/or chalcid wasps to the garden. Use derris only as a last resort for the most serious infestations.

BEAN BEETLE brownish orange wings covered with evenly spaced black spots, shiny black head and legs, $\frac{1}{4}$ in (6 mm) long. The larva is a white grub, less than $\frac{1}{4}$ in (6 mm) long. Signs: furrows chewed into leaves.

BUFF TIP MOTH moth with wingspan of $2\frac{1}{2}$ in (6 cm) and buff tips on the forewing. The larvae, up to $1\frac{1}{2}$ in (4 cm) are more often seen, living in groups. They can defoliate apple, cherry and cobnuts. Physically destroy larvae as soon as spotted, or dust with derris.

CABBAGE MOTH brownish-grey moth with a silver splotch near the middle of each forewing, $1\frac{1}{2}$ in (4 cm) long. Larva is a pale green caterpillar with a white line on each side, $1\frac{1}{2}$ in (4 cm) long. Introduce trichogramma wasps. For serious infestations apply bacillus thuringiensis.

▲ The caterpillar of the small white is a common pest of cabbages, but unlike the large white, the caterpillars hide in the heart of the cabbage.

CABBAGE ROOT FLY a grey fly with black stripes along its thorax, $\frac{1}{4}$ in (6 mm) long. The larva (cabbage maggot) is a white maggot, less than $\frac{1}{4}$ in (6 mm) long. Signs: wilting plants when water available. Lay paper around base of seedling.

CABBAGE WHITE BUTTERFLY large white-cream coloured butterfly with a $1\frac{1}{2}$ in (4 cm) wingspan. The larvae is greenish-yellow and feeds on members of the cabbage family. Control by physically destroying groups of eggs, and picking off caterpillars. Dust with derris.

CARROT ROOT FLY a major pest on carrots, parsnips, parsley and celery. The larva, up to $\frac{1}{2}$ in (1.3 cm) long bores through the developing carrot. Planting seeds after May will avoid the insect life cycle. If planting before, erect barrier up to two feet tall to deter flies from detecting carrots by smell.

▲ Harmful: Whitegrubs eat through plant roots which kills the plants. They are difficult to remove, but turning the soil brings a few to the surface for birds to eat.

◀ Harmful: Wireworms or mealworms can be a major pest. They are best removed from lawns by rolling, which squashes them in the soil, or by turning them up in the soil for birds to eat.

CODLING MOTH is bown-black with ½ in (1.3 cm) wingspan. It is a serious pest of apples, and to a lesser extent pears. Eggs laid in flowers hatch as caterpillars which feed on the inside of the developing fruit. Tie sacking round tree trunk in the autumn to trap over-wintering caterpillars, then kill them.

CURRANT CLEARWING MOTH has transparent wings and is wasp-like with a wingspan up to 6/8th in (1.6 cm) long. The larvae which are 5/8th in (1.5 cm) long are stem-borers and attack black currant, red currant and gooseberry plants. Infected wood must be cut out and burnt.

CUTWORM moth with mottled shades of grey and brown, 1½ in (4 cm). Larva is a grey-brown caterpillar with darker spots along its sides, 1–2 in (2.5–4 cm). Sign: seedling stems cut just above or below ground level. Encircle the seedling stem with a paper or cardboard collar. Introduce trichogramma wasps. Bacillus thuringiensis for more severe problems.

◀ **Harmful: Mealy cabbage aphids infest the undersides of leaves of cabbage, Brussels sprout buttons and the hearts of cauliflowers. They live in dense colonies and feed on the sap, causing the leaf eventually to go yellow. As the aphid overwinters as on egg on the stems of these plants, remove, bury or burn old stalks.**

EARWIGS are about ½ in (1.3 cm) long, brown, with ineffectual pincers on the end of their bodies. They are pests on dahlias and chrysanthemum flowers where they eat the petals. They are controlled by physically looking for them and destroying them.

FLEA BEETLE shiny black beetle with two curved yellow stripes along its wing covers that give the central black area an hourglass appearance, 1/10 in. Sign: tiny holes chewed in leaves. Dust with derris.

FRIT FLY a two-wing fly, dark grey to black, 1/8th of an inch long. The white maggots feed inside the shoots of sweet corn and destroy the leaves. Female frit flies only lay their eggs on shoots which have five or less leaves, so grow seedlings in greenhouse where frit flies will not find them, before planting out.

▶ **Harmful: The black bean aphid is the only aphid species which will feed on beans and it causes plenty of damage wherever it feeds, such as distorted growth and loss of beans.**

GHOST SWIFT MOTH a ghostly shiny white, wingspan up to 2 in (5 cm), whitish larva up to 2½ in (6 cm) long. The female broadcasts her eggs over plants and is impossible to control. Cream-coloured larvae live up to three years and eat the roots of grasses as well as raspberry, strawberry and hop.

LEAFHOPPER wedged-shaped insect with small pointed head, less than ¼ in (6 mm), nearly every colour of the rainbow in one species or another. Sign: stunted and discoloured leaves and stems. Spray from plants with strong burst of water.

LEAFMINER a black fly with bright yellow stripes on body and dark, translucent wings, 1/10 in. Larva is a tiny yellowish worm. Sign: white tunnels inside leaves. Remove all the infested leaves.

LILY BEETLE is about 3/8th of an inch long, bright red with black legs. They and their orange-red larvae defoliate lily leaves, flowers and fruit capsules. Dust with derris.

NARCICUSS BULB FLY the white-cream larvae which grows to ¾ in (2 cm) long causes damage inside the bulb by eating it out. Daffodils, snowdrops, onions and beans are attacked. The fly lays its eggs on the neck of the bulbs, so dust with derris and rake up old leaves around bulbs.

ONION FLY grey, hump-backed fly with large, red-brown eyes and blue, translucent wings, 1/4 in (6 mm). Larva is a white grub, less than 1/4 in (6 mm). Sign: tunnels in onion bulbs.

PEA AND BEAN WEEVIL about 1/4 of an inch long, grey-brown, which eats notches from the sides of pea and broad bean leaves. Becomes a pest in early summer. Dust with derris.

SLUG AND SNAIL slimy, brown to black creatures with two protruding eye-tentacles, 1/2–3 in (1–7 cm); snails have hard shells. Sign: holes chewed in centres of leaves. A shallow saucer of

◀ **Harmful: Slugs, above, and snails, below, are closely related garden pests, particularly on leaf crops like lettuce.**

stale beer placed on the ground will attract, trap and drown them.

SMALL WHITE BUTTERFLY with a black tip and two or three black spots on each wing, 1–2 in (2.5–5 cm). Larva is a pale green caterpillar with yellow stripes along its sides, 1 1/4 in (3 cm). Spray infested area with sour milk or garlic water. Introduce trichogramma wasps.

STRAWBERRY FRUIT WEEVIL brown to black and shiny beetles up to 2/8th of an inch long. The pale larvae attack strawberry and raspberry and can be controlled with derris dust.

THRIP without magnification, an infestation of thrip looks like a series of thin, black lines running across the leaves. Dust with derris dust.

Beneficial Insects

▲ **Beneficial: Although the lacewings are not nearly as well-known as ladybird beetles and praying mantii, they are another environmentally friendly, natural garden pest deterrent.**

▲ **Beneficial: Toads consume a great many insects every night. Unfortunately, they do not discriminate between harmful and beneficial insects. Earthworms can make up a sizeable proportion of their diet.**

▲ **Beneficial: Honeybees visit tens of thousands of flowers in order to make a single pound of honey and, in doing so, pass the pollen from one plant to another thus transferring pollen.**

VINE WEEVIL dark beetles, about ⅜th of an inch long, and nocturnal in their habits. The light-coloured larvae up to ⅜th of an inch long cause more damage to strawberry, currants and gooseberry than the adult beetle. Control by dusting with derris. Mature plants are more resistant to attack than young ones.

WHITEFLY white, angular fly with a powdery appearance, less than 1⁄10 in. Nymph is even smaller, green, translucent. Sign: weakened, wilting plants. Encarsia formosa will parasitize the whitefly nymphs.

WIREWORM grey to brown moth with scattered, darker spots, less than ½ in (6 mm). Larva looks a lot like a small, reddish orange mealy worm, ¼–⅓ in (6 mm). Sign: chewed roots, tubers, seeds. Small pieces of potato scattered about the garden will trap the worms for easy removal.

Weeds

Any weeds that might appear are handled in the same manner, although with the techniques outlined in this book the chances of weeds shoving in close to your crop plants are much reduced. But for those that do appear, simply grasp them as close to ground level as possible and pull. Care must be exercised if the weed is growing close to your crop plant – pulling may damage the roots of the plant you want to retain.

Nobody enjoys weeding. Accept that fact and move beyond it. As a matter of fact, you might cheer yourself a bit with the knowledge that you've reduced your weeding choice anywhere from 50 to 80 per cent by leaving the conventional row-type garden in your past. The reduction in overall garden space that our techniques result in have led to a natural and corresponding reduction in space claimed by weeds.

But, even more so, many of the techniques outlined here contribute to lower weed levels, even if applied to a row-type garden. For example, you're now growing your crop plants closer together than ever before. As they reach maturity and their leaves come into contact with one another, they provide some of their own defence against weed growth by robbing young weeds below them of the necessities for growth.

So, don't put off the weeding chore. Attack while the weeds are still small and tender. Similar to your tender, young crop seedlings, weed seedlings are more susceptible to all forms of attack, including any damage you can do to them.

▲ Birds are often a welcome garden guest but they can also be a pest. Protect fruit crops with netting and crop seedlings with cage wire tunnels.

Bigger pests

Animal and bird pests represent another level of attack on your garden crops. The best defence for small garden spaces like we've been discussing is enclosure. Rabbits are easily deterred by any fencing that stands just a couple of feet tall and has openings small enough to keep them out (less than three inches square). Birds are best handled by the cage wire tunnels that we described earlier. Their threat is mostly past when the plants grow beyond the seed and seedling stage.

Smaller, but deadly

The most difficult garden problems are the various diseases. Even with the close and steady surveillance that your new gardening methods encourage, it is often too late to do much about diseases once you've noticed them.

Prevention is the key to control over garden diseases. You're starting with a rich, healthy soil and similarly healthy plants, disease-resistant varieties as much as possible. You're applying water and fertilizers at ground level, rather than wetting the plant leaves. You're removing weeds almost as soon as they poke their heads through the soil. And, you're rotating your crops so as never to raise the same family of plant in the same space back-to-back.

And yet, some disease problems are nearly inevitable. In many cases, your most effective reaction when you notice the symptoms is the quick removal of the infected plant. Remove it entirely from the garden environment. Do not add it to the compost pile.

▲ Harmful: Early blight is just one of the very many diseases that can strike garden crops, often with no obvious warning.

▲ As autumn approaches, your thoughts may begin to wander away from gardening towards other pursuits. But there's still some work to be done outdoors.

As autumn approaches

Although you may be planning to extend your growing season beyond the first few frosts of autumn, the approach of autumn is nonetheless a critical time in all gardens.

You probably still have several summer crops in significant production, including beans, sweetcorn, cucumbers, aubergines, squash, Swiss chard and tomatoes. Similarly, second, late-summer plantings of crops like beetroot, broccoli, cabbage, carrots, cauliflower, lettuce, and spinach are now reaching the harvest stage.

You will want to harvest as much of the crop from all of these plants just as quickly as possible. Make certain that all the plants are putting their full energy into ripening their vegetables. All new growth of stem and leaf should be thwarted as swiftly as possible by strong pruning. Water should be cut off at this point.

As you get closer to that fateful first frost, you may want to lay the vining crops that are still producing into a shallow, straw-lined trench and cover them with a plastic-covered wire tunnel as described earlier in the book. Another option, if your remaining crops are relatively close together, is to cover the entire garden with a plastic tarpaulin each evening. Be sure to remove the tarpaulin the following morning.

▲ The weeks just before the first frosts are critical in getting the maximum harvest from the garden before the crop is lost. Tomatoes, for example, must be pushed to ripen as much fruit as quickly as possible. They can also be picked and placed on the windowsill in the sun to ripen.

At this time of the year you might also be getting ready to plant new crops of winter lettuce and radishes directly into the garden. Of course, if you started the lettuce seeds indoors about four weeks earlier, you will be that many weeks ahead of the game.

Your portable cold frame, triple-stacked, is in place with a rich mixture of soil and fertilizer inside. Plantings of lettuce, spinach, kale, carrots and radishes into the frame should provide you with harvestable crops well into winter. Add extra insulation around the outside of the frame with bales of straw snugged up against it. If you've placed the frame near the southern side of your home, it will draw some extra radiated heat for some time to come. You might also want to place large rocks throughout the inside of the frame on top of the soil. These will collect whatever heat the sun gives up during the day and radiate some of it into the air space of the frame at night.

Whatever soil you're no longer using for growing plants should be prepared now, as explained in our chapter on soil. A good, extra-thick mulch should then be applied on top of it.

This is also the time of year to sort through your left-over gardening supplies. Your seeds should be safely stored in the refrigerator, but other supplies like fertilizer, lime, peat moss and the like probably still need your attention. They can be stored in dry, sealed containers for use next spring, with no loss in quality.

However, any that are showing the signs of moisture penetration in the form of hardness and large lumps, should probably be added to the compost pile. You'll need some "activators" for all the leaves you'll probably be adding at this time of year, anyway.

Autumn is also a good time to begin thinking about building any of the devices described in this book that you haven't already put together. The coming months are going to be rather sparse when it comes to garden-related activity.

And, finally, it's time to start relying more heavily once again on the local farmer's market. Luckily for those fresh produce lovers, many of these continue to operate throughout the winter. Don't forget to keep an eye peeled for new ideas.

▲ Late summer and early autumn can give the most bountiful harvests of the entire gardening season, and you can feel proud of the fruits of your labours.

Plant directory

Asparagus

Asparagus officinalis

Liliaceae, Lily Family

GROWING SEASON: *Perennial; early spring crop.*

SPACING: *12 in (30 cm).*

ROOT DEPTH: *4 feet and more.*

BREADTH AT MATURITY: *2–4 ft (60–120 cm).*

HEIGHT AT MATURITY: *3–8 ft (91–240 cm).*

SEED TO HARVEST: *3 years.*

SPRING PLANTING: *Start seeds or transplant outdoors 2–4 weeks before last frost.*

PH REQUIREMENT: *6.0 to 8.0*

SUNLIGHT REQUIREMENT: *Full sun.*

INITIAL FERTILIZER: *Phosphorus and potassium before planting, nitrogen after.*

IN-SEASON FERTILIZER: *Twice a year.*

WATER REQUIREMENT: *Heavy.*

PESTS/DISEASES: *Asparagus beetle; fusarium wilt.*

SPECIAL ATTENTION: *Do not harvest in first two seasons. Angle several inches of compost to the plants each spring.*

HARVEST: *8–10 weeks per plant. Begin when spears are 3/8 in or more in diameter.*

Beans (Broad)

Vicia faba

Leguminosae, Pea Family

GROWING SEASON: *Summer.*

SPACING: *3 in (7 cm).*

ROOT DEPTH: *36 in (91 cm) and more.*

BREADTH AT MATURITY: *4–8 in (10–20 cm).*

HEIGHT AT MATURITY: *10–24 in (25–61 cm).*

SEED TO HARVEST: *8 weeks.*

SPRING PLANTING: *Start seeds outdoors on date of last frost.*

STAGGERED PLANTING: *Every 2–4 weeks.*

PH REQUIREMENT: *6.2 to 7.5.*

SUNLIGHT REQUIREMENT: *Full sun.*

INITIAL FERTILIZER: *Low nitrogen, moderate phosphorus and potassium.*

IN-SEASON FERTILIZER: *After flowers appear.*

WATER REQUIREMENT: *Medium.*

PESTS/DISEASES: *Aphids, cabbage moth, leafminers,
anthracnose, bacterial blight, bacterial spot, downy mildew, mosaics, rust.*

SPECIAL ATTENTION: *Apply bacterial inoculant powder before planting.*

HARVEST: *When plant's leaves have fallen, but before first frost.*

BEANS (BUTTERBEAN)

Phaseolus limensis

Leguminosae, Pea Family

GROWING SEASON: *Summer.*

SPACING: *4 in (10 cm).*

ROOT DEPTH: *36 in (91 cm) and more, if grown vertically.*

BREADTH AT MATURITY: *Trailing, 6–8 in (15–20 cm).*
Bush, 4–6 in (10–15 cm).

HEIGHT AT MATURITY: *Trailing, 7–15 ft (2–5 m), if grown vertically.*
Bush, 12–18 in (30–46 cm).

SEED TO HARVEST: *8 weeks.*

SPRING PLANTING: *Start seeds outdoors on date of last frost.*

STAGGERED PLANTING: *Every 2–4 weeks.*

PH REQUIREMENT: *6.0 to 7.0.*

SUNLIGHT REQUIREMENT: *Full sun.*

INITIAL FERTILIZER: *Low nitrogen, moderate phosphorus and potassium.*

IN-SEASON FERTILIZER: *4 weeks after planting.*

WATER REQUIREMENT: *Medium.*

PESTS/DISEASES: *Aphids, cabbage moth, leafminers,*
anchracnose, bacterial blight, bacterial spot, downy mildew, mosaics, rust.

SPECIAL ATTENTION: *Apply bacterial inoculant powder before planting.*

HARVEST: *As beans bulge against pods.*

BEANS (FRENCH)

Phaseolus vulgaris

Leguminosae, Pea Family

GROWING SEASON: *Summer.*

SPACING: *4 in (10 cm).*

ROOT DEPTH: *36 in (91 cm) and more.*

BREADTH AT MATURITY: *Trailing, 6–8 in (15–18 cm), if grown vertically.*
Bush, 4–6 in (10–15 cm).

HEIGHT AT MATURITY: *Trailing, 7–15 ft (2–5 m), if grown vertically.*
Bush, 1–2 ft (30–60 cm).

SEED TO HARVEST: *8 weeks.*

SPRING PLANTING: *Start seeds outdoors on date of last frost.*

STAGGERED PLANTING: *Every 2–4 weeks.*

PH REQUIREMENT: *6.2 to 7.5.*

SUNLIGHT REQUIREMENT: *Full sun.*

INITIAL FERTILIZER: *Low nitrogen, moderate phosphorus and potassium.*

IN-SEASON FERTILIZER: *When flowers appear.*

WATER REQUIREMENT: *Medium.*

PESTS/DISEASES: *Aphids, cabbage moth, leafminers,*
anthracnose, bacterial blight, bacterial spot, downy mildew, mosaics, rust.

SPECIAL ATTENTION: *Apply bacterial inoculant powder before planting.*

HARVEST: *When pods snap in half cleanly; before beans bulge against pods.*

BEETROOT

Beta vulgaris

Chenopodiaceae, Goosefoot Family

GROWING SEASON: *Spring–autumn.*

SPACING: *3–4 in (7–10 cm).*

ROOT DEPTH: *24 in (60 cm) and more.*

BREADTH AT MATURITY: *4–8 in (10–20 cm).*

HEIGHT AT MATURITY: *10–14 in (25–36 cm).*

SEED TO HARVEST: *8 weeks.*

SPRING PLANTING: *Start seeds outdoors 4 weeks before last frost.*

STAGGERED PLANTING: *Every 2–4 weeks.*

PH REQUIREMENT: 5.8–7.0

SUNLIGHT REQUIREMENT: *Full to partial sun.*

INITIAL FERTILIZER: *High phosphorus, low nitrogen.*

IN-SEASON FERTILIZER: *Every 2 weeks, low nitrogen.*

WATER REQUIREMENT: *Medium.*

PESTS/DISEASES: *Aphids, leafhoppers, leafminers, slugs, snails; leaf spot.*

SPECIAL ATTENTION: *Choose quick-maturing, bolt-resistant varieties; never apply fresh manure.*

HARVEST: *When beetroot 1–2 in (2–5 cm) in diameter.*

BROCCOLI

Brassica oleracae, Botrytis Group

Brassicaceae, Mustard Family

GROWING SEASON: *Spring, autumn.*

SPACING: *15 in (38 cm).*

ROOT DEPTH: *18 in (46 cm) and more.*

BREADTH AT MATURITY: *16–24 in (41–61 cm).*

HEIGHT AT MATURITY: *1½ to 4 ft (46–122 cm).*

SEED TO HARVEST: *16 weeks.*

SPRING PLANTING: *Start seeds indoors 12 weeks before last frost. Transplant outdoors 6 weeks before last frost.*

AUTUMN PLANTING: *Start seeds indoors 6 weeks after last spring frost. Transplant outdoors 8 weeks before first frost.*

PH REQUIREMENT: 6.0–7.5.

SUNLIGHT REQUIREMENT: *Full sun.*

INITIAL FERTILIZER: *Moderate nitrogen and phosphorus.*

IN-SEASON FERTILIZER: *When buds form.*

WATER REQUIREMENT: *Medium.*

PESTS/DISEASES: *Cutworms, flea beetles, aphids, cabbage moth, cabbage fly, leafminers; black rot, clubroot, small white caterpillar, large white caterpillar.*

SPECIAL ATTENTION: *The heads go to flower and lose food value fast in the heat; don't compost any part of these plants; rotate location widely.*

HARVEST: *When head about 4 in (10 cm) in diameter, no more.*

BRUSSELS SPROUTS

Brassica oleracae, Gemmifera Group

Brassicaceae, Mustard Family

GROWING SEASON: *Spring, autumn.*

SPACING: *12 in (30 cm).*

ROOT DEPTH: *18 in (46 cm) and more.*

BREADTH AT MATURITY: *20–28 in (50–70 cm).*

HEIGHT AT MATURITY: *2–4 ft (60–120 cm).*

SEED TO HARVEST: *16 weeks.*

SPRING PLANTING: *Start seeds indoors 5 weeks before last frost. Transplant outdoors on date of last frost.*

AUTUMN PLANTING: *Start seeds indoors 16 weeks before first fall frost. Transplant outdoors 11 weeks before first frost.*

PH REQUIREMENT: *6.0–7.5*

SUNLIGHT REQUIREMENT: *Full sun.*

INITIAL FERTILIZER: *Moderate phosphorus, high potassium.*

IN-SEASON FERTILIZER: *2 weeks after transplanting; every 4 weeks thereafter.*

WATER REQUIREMENT: *Medium.*

PESTS/DISEASES: *Aphids, cutworms, flea beetles, cabbage moth, cabbage fly, leafminers; clubroot, small white caterpillar, large white caterpillar.*

SPECIAL ATTENTION: *As a sprout bulges remove the leaf below it; don't compost any part of these plants; rotate location widely.*

HARVEST: *When sprouts about 1 in (2.5 cm) in diameter, no more; harvest from bottom of plant upwards.*

CABBAGE

Brassica oleracae, Capitata Group

Brassicaceae, Mustard Family

GROWING SEASON: *Spring, autumn.*

SPACING: *12 in (30 cm).*

ROOT DEPTH: *12 in (30 cm) and more.*

BREADTH AT MATURITY: *24–42 in (60–107 cm).*

HEIGHT AT MATURITY: *12–16 in (30–41 cm).*

SEED TO HARVEST: *16 weeks.*

SPRING PLANTING: *Start seeds indoors 12 weeks before last frost. Transplant outdoors 4–6 weeks before last frost.*

AUTUMN PLANTING: *Start seeds indoors 16 weeks before first fall frost. Transplant outdoors 8 weeks before first frost.*

PH REQUIREMENT: *6.0–7.5.*

SUNLIGHT REQUIREMENT: *Full sun.*

INITIAL FERTILIZER: *Moderate nitrogen and phosphorus, high potassium.*

IN-SEASON FERTILIZER: *Every 2 weeks.*

WATER REQUIREMENT: *Heavy early in season; medium rest of time.*

PESTS/DISEASES: *Aphids, cabbage moth, cabbage fly, cutworms, flea beetles, harlequin bugs, leafminers; downy mildew.*

SPECIAL ATTENTION: *Don't compost any part of these plants; rotate location widely.*

HARVEST: *When heads much smaller than those commonly found in supermarkets, for best flavour.*

CARROT

Daucus carota v. sativum

Umbelliferae, Parsley Family

GROWING SEASON: *Year-round.*

SPACING: *3 in (7 cm).*

ROOT DEPTH: *18 in (46 cm) and more.*

BREADTH AT MATURITY: *12–24 in (30–60 cm).*

HEIGHT AT MATURITY: *12–16 in (30–40 cm).*

SEED TO HARVEST: *10 weeks.*

SPRING PLANTING: *Start seeds outdoors 4 weeks before last frost.*

AUTUMN PLANTING: *Start seeds outdoors until 2 weeks before first frost.*

STAGGERED PLANTING: *Every 2–4 weeks.*

PH REQUIREMENT: *5.5–6.5.*

SUNLIGHT REQUIREMENT: *Full to partial sun.*

INITIAL FERTILIZER: *Low nitrogen, moderate phosphorus, high potassium.*

IN-SEASON FERTILIZER: *3 weeks after seeds germinate; when tops 6 in (15 cm) tall.*

WATER REQUIREMENT: *Medium.*

PESTS/DISEASES: *Aphids, cutworms; leaf blight, root knot nematode, carrot fly.*

SPECIAL ATTENTION: *Loose, friable soil is essential.*

HARVEST: *When less than 1½ in (4 cm) in diameter.*

CAULIFLOWER

Brassica oleracae, Botrytis Group

Brassicaceae, Mustard Family

GROWING SEASON: *Spring, autumn.*

SPACING: *12 in (30 cm).*

ROOT DEPTH: *18 in (46 cm) and more.*

BREADTH AT MATURITY: *23–32 in (60–81 cm).*

HEIGHT AT MATURITY: *18–24 in (46–61 cm).*

SEED TO HARVEST: *14 weeks.*

SPRING PLANTING: *Start seeds indoors 10 weeks before last frost. Transplant outdoors 4 weeks before last frost, with nighttime covers until date of last frost.*

AUTUMN PLANTING: *Start seeds indoors 8 weeks after last spring frost. Transplant outdoors 8 weeks before first frost.*

PH REQUIREMENT: *6.0–7.5.*

SUNLIGHT REQUIREMENT: *Full sun.*

INITIAL FERTILIZER: *Low nitrogen, moderate phosphorus and potassium.*

IN-SEASON FERTILIZER: *Every 3 weeks.*

WATER REQUIREMENT: *Medium.*

PESTS/DISEASES: *Aphids, cabbage moth, cabbage fly, cutworms, flea beetles, leafminers; black rot, clubroot, small white caterpillars, large white caterpillars.*

SPECIAL ATTENTION: *The heads bolt quickly in the heat; when heads start forming, tie the leaves over them to prevent their yellowing; don't compost.*

HARVEST: *When head 8–10 in (20–25 cm) in diameter.*

CORN (SWEET)

Zea mays v. rugosa,

Graminae, Grass Family

GROWING SEASON: *Summer.*

SPACING: *12 in (30 cm).*

ROOT DEPTH: *18 in (46 cm) and more.*

BREADTH AT MATURITY: *18–48 in (46–122 cm).*

HEIGHT AT MATURITY: *5–7 ft (152–210 cm).*

SEED TO HARVEST: *9–14 weeks.*

SPRING PLANTING: *Plant seeds outdoors on the date of the last frost.*

STAGGERED PLANTING: *Every 2–4 weeks.*

PH REQUIREMENT: *5.5–7.0.*

SUNLIGHT REQUIREMENT: *Full sun.*

INITIAL FERTILIZER: *High nitrogen and phosphorus, moderate potassium.*

IN-SEASON FERTILIZER: *When stalks are 12 in (30 cm) tall and again when 24 in (60 cm) tall; also every 2 weeks.*

WATER REQUIREMENT: *Medium.*

PESTS/DISEASES: *Bacterial wilt, corn smut.*

SPECIAL ATTENTION: *Must be planted in multiple rows to facilitate pollination; seeds and seedlings need protection from birds; shallow roots require heavy mulch.*

HARVEST: *When head about 4 in (10 cm) in diameter, no more.*

CUCUMBERS

Cucumis sativus

Cucurbitaceae, Gourd Family

GROWING SEASON: *Summer.*

SPACING: *8 in (20 cm).*

ROOT DEPTH: *24 in (60 cm) and more.*

BREADTH AT MATURITY: *12–16 in (30–41 cm) when grown vertical.*

HEIGHT AT MATURITY: *6 ft (183 cm).*

SEED TO HARVEST: *9 weeks.*

SPRING PLANTING: *Start seeds indoors 2 weeks before last frost. Transplant outdoors 1–2 weeks after last frost. Plant seeds outdoors 1 week after last frost, for mid- to late-summer harvest. Plant seeds or transplant outdoors 8 weeks after last spring frost for harvest up to first autumn frost.*

PH REQUIREMENT: *5.5–7.0.*

SUNLIGHT REQUIREMENT: *Full sun.*

INITIAL FERTILIZER: *Moderate nitrogen and potassium, high phosphorus.*

IN-SEASON FERTILIZER: *Every 2 weeks.*

WATER REQUIREMENT: *Medium; when producing fruit, heavy.*

PESTS/DISEASES: *Aphids, anthracnose, bacterial wilt, downy mildew, mosaic, powdery mildew.*

SPECIAL ATTENTION: *Shallow roots are easily damaged by close cultivation.*

HARVEST: *For fresh use pick at 6–10 in (15–25 cm) in length; for pickling pick at 4–6 in (10–15 cm).*

EGGPLANT — AUBERGINE

Solanum melongena v. esculentum

Solanaceae, Nightshade Family

GROWING SEASON: *Summer.*

SPACING: *12 in (30 cm).*

ROOT DEPTH: *36 in (91 cm) and more.*

BREADTH AT MATURITY: *2–4 ft (60–122 cm).*

HEIGHT AT MATURITY: *2–3 ft (60–91 cm).*

SEED TO HARVEST: *19 weeks.*

SPRING PLANTING: *Start seeds indoors 8 weeks before last frost. Transplant outdoors 2 weeks after last frost.*

PH REQUIREMENT: *5.5–6.5.*

SUNLIGHT REQUIREMENT: *Full sun.*

INITIAL FERTILIZER: *Moderate nitrogen and potassium.*

IN-SEASON FERTILIZER: *When first fruit forms.*

WATER REQUIREMENT: *Heavy.*

PESTS/DISEASES: *Aphids, cutworms, flea beetles, leafhoppers, fruit rot, verticillium wilt.*

SPECIAL ATTENTION: *As soon as the soil has fully warmed for the season, surround the plant with thick mulch; all parts of the plant other than fruit are poisonous.*

HARVEST: *When fruit about 4 in (10 cm) in diameter, before lustre disappears from fruit.*

ENDIVE

Cichorium endivia

Compositae, Sunflower Family

GROWING SEASON: *Year-round.*

SPACING: *8 in (20 cm).*

ROOT DEPTH: *6 in (15 cm) and more.*

BREADTH AT MATURITY: *8–12 in (20–30 cm).*

HEIGHT AT MATURITY: *12–18 in (30–46 cm).*

SEED TO HARVEST: *12 weeks.*

SPRING PLANTING: *Start seeds indoors 4 weeks before last frost. Transplant outdoors on date of last frost. Plant seeds outdoors 3 weeks before last frost.*

AUTUMN PLANTING: *Start seeds indoors 15 weeks after last spring frost. Transplant outdoors 11 weeks before first frost.*

STAGGERED PLANTING: *Every 2–4 weeks.*

PH REQUIREMENT: *6.0–7.0.*

SUNLIGHT REQUIREMENT: *Full sun.*

INITIAL FERTILIZER: *Moderate nitrogen and potassium.*

IN-SEASON FERTILIZER: *When plants about ⅓ mature.*

WATER REQUIREMENT: *Heavy.*

PESTS/DISEASES: *Aphids, cabbage moth, cutworms, flea beetles, leafminers, slugs, snails; bacterial diseases, lettuce rot.*

SPECIAL ATTENTION: *Blanch heads to avoid bitterness.*

HARVEST: *When head begins to turn whitish at base.*

GARLIC

Allium sativum

Liliaceae, Lily Family

GROWING SEASON: *Spring.*

SPACING: *6 in (15 cm).*

ROOT DEPTH: *2 in (5 cm) and more.*

BREADTH AT MATURITY: *6–10 in (15–25 cm).*

HEIGHT AT MATURITY: *12–36 in (30–91 cm).*

SEED TO HARVEST: *(Plant as clove) 16 weeks.*

SPRING PLANTING: *Plant cloves outdoors 4 weeks before last frost.*

PH REQUIREMENT: *4.5–8.3*

SUNLIGHT REQUIREMENT: *Full sun.*

INITIAL FERTILIZER: *Moderate nitrogen, phosphorus and potassium.*

IN-SEASON FERTILIZER: *Not needed.*

WATER REQUIREMENT: *Low, none during summer.*

PESTS/DISEASES: *Onion fly, thrips; downy mildew, neck rot, pink rot, smut.*

SPECIAL ATTENTION: *Remove any flower heads that develop.*

HARVEST: *When tops turn brown and die off on their own.*

KALE

Brassica oleracea v. acephela

Brassicaceae, Mustard Family

GROWING SEASON: *Year-round.*

SPACING: *12 in (30 cm).*

ROOT DEPTH: *6 in (15 cm) and more.*

BREADTH AT MATURITY: *8–12 in (20–30 cm).*

HEIGHT AT MATURITY: *12–18 in (30–46 cm).*

SEED TO HARVEST: *12 weeks.*

SPRING PLANTING: *Start seeds indoors 4 weeks before last frost. Transplant outdoors on date of last frost. Plant seeds outdoors 3 weeks before last frost.*

AUTUMN PLANTING: *Start seeds indoors 15 weeks after last spring frost. Transplant outdoors 11 weeks before first frost.*

STAGGERED PLANTING: *Every 4 weeks.*

PH REQUIREMENT: *6.0–7.0.*

SUNLIGHT REQUIREMENT: *Full to partial sun.*

INITIAL FERTILIZER: *High potassium.*

IN-SEASON FERTILIZER: *When plants about one-third mature.*

WATER REQUIREMENT: *Heavy.*

PESTS/DISEASES: *Aphids, cabbage moth, cabbage fly, cabbage worms, cutworms, flea beetles, harlequin bugs, leafminers; black rot, small white caterpillar, large white caterpillar.*

SPECIAL ATTENTION: *Don't compost any parts of these plants; rotate widely.*

HARVEST: *As soon as leaves are large enough to warrant their use; harvest from the middle and retain some leaves at bottom to feed new growth.*

KOHLRABI

Brassica oleracea

Brassicaceae, Mustard Family

GROWING SEASON: *Spring.*

SPACING: *6 in (15 cm).*

ROOT DEPTH: *12 in (30 cm) and more.*

BREADTH AT MATURITY: *6–12 in (15–30 cm).*

HEIGHT AT MATURITY: *6–12 in (15–30 cm).*

SEED TO HARVEST: *9 weeks.*

SPRING PLANTING: *Plant seeds indoors 10 weeks before last frost. Transplant outdoors 5 weeks before last frost. Plant seeds outdoors 5 weeks before last frost.*

AUTUMN PLANTING: *Plant seeds or transplant outdoors 10 weeks before first frost.*

STAGGERED PLANTING: *Every 2–3 weeks.*

PH REQUIREMENT: *6.0–7.5.*

SUNLIGHT REQUIREMENT: *Full sun.*

INITIAL FERTILIZER: *Low nitrogen, phosphorus and potassium.*

IN-SEASON FERTILIZER: *Every 4 weeks.*

WATER REQUIREMENT: *Medium.*

PESTS/DISEASES: *Aphids, cabbage moth, cutworms, flea beetles, leafminers, slugs, snails; black rot.*

HARVEST: *When bulge reaches diameter of 1–2 in (2.5–5 cm), nothing larger.*

LEEKS

Allium ampeloprasum

Liliaceae, Lily Family

GROWING SEASON: *Spring, summer.*

SPACING: *5 in (12 cm).*

ROOT DEPTH: *12 in (30 cm) and more.*

BREADTH AT MATURITY: *6–12 in (15–30 cm).*

HEIGHT AT MATURITY: *15–30 in (38–76 cm).*

SEED TO HARVEST: *19 weeks.*

SPRING PLANTING: *Plant seeds indoors 9 weeks before last frost. Transplant outdoors 5 weeks before last frost. Plant seeds outdoors 5 weeks before last frost.*

STAGGERED PLANTING: *Every 2 weeks.*

PH REQUIREMENT: *6.0–7.5.*

SUNLIGHT REQUIREMENT: *Full sun.*

INITIAL FERTILIZER: *Low nitrogen, phosphorus and potassium.*

IN-SEASON FERTILIZER: *Every 4 weeks.*

WATER REQUIREMENT: *Medium.*

PESTS/DISEASES: *Onion fly, thrips; downy mildew, neck rot, pink rot, smut.*

HARVEST: *When bulb is 1–2 in (2.5–5 cm) in diameter, not later.*

LETTUCE

Lactuca sativa

Compositae, Sunflower Family

GROWING SEASON: *Year-round.*

SPACING: *6 in (15 cm).*

ROOT DEPTH: *12 in (30 cm) and more.*

BREADTH AT MATURITY: *6–12 in (15–30 cm).*

HEIGHT AT MATURITY: *6–12 in (15–30 cm).*

SEED TO HARVEST: *7 weeks.*

SPRING PLANTING: *Plant seeds indoors 8 weeks before last frost. Transplant outdoors 4 weeks before last frost. Plant seeds outdoors 4 weeks before last frost.*

AUTUMN PLANTING: *Plant seeds of transplant outdoors 8 weeks before first frost.*

STAGGERED PLANTING: *Every 2–3 weeks.*

PH REQUIREMENT: *6.5–7.5.*

SUNLIGHT REQUIREMENT: *Partial sun.*

INITIAL FERTILIZER: *Low nitrogen, phosphorus and potassium.*

IN-SEASON FERTILIZER: *Every 2 weeks.*

WATER REQUIREMENT: *Low to medium.*

PESTS/DISEASES: *Aphids, cabbage moth, cutworms, flea beetles, leafminers, slugs, snails; bacteria, fungus, lettuce rot.*

SPECIAL ATTENTION: *During hot weather shade is a must.*

HARVEST: *For salad bowl lettuce, when you have a half-dozen leaves of 2 in (5 cm) or more. For head lettuce, when the round head feels firm. All lettuces have better taste if harvested early in the morning.*

MELON

(including cantaloupe)

Cucumis melo, Reticulatus Group

Cucurbitaceae, Gourd Family

GROWING SEASON: *Summer.*

SPACING: *12 in (30 cm).*

ROOT DEPTH: *6 in (15 cm) and more.*

BREADTH AT MATURITY: *24–36 in (60–91 cm), when grown vertically.*

HEIGHT AT MATURITY: *7 ft (2.10 m), when grown vertically.*

SEED TO HARVEST: *12 weeks.*

SPRING PLANTING: *Plant seeds indoors on date of last frost. Transplant outdoors 2–4 weeks after last frost. Plant seeds outdoors 2–4 weeks after last frost.*

PH REQUIREMENT: *6.0–6.5.*

SUNLIGHT REQUIREMENT: *Full sun.*

INITIAL FERTILIZER: *Moderate nitrogen, phosphorus and potassium.*

IN-SEASON FERTILIZER: *Every 4 weeks.*

WATER REQUIREMENT: *Medium, but no water when fruit starts to turn ripe.*

PESTS/DISEASES: *Cutworms; mildew, wilt.*

SPECIAL ATTENTION: *Be very careful around the roots; when fruit begins to develop pinch off the plant to two leaves beyond fruit; rinds are excellent compost.*

HARVEST: *When fruit "slips" easily off stem.*

ONIONS

Allium cepa

Liliaceae, Lily Family

GROWING SEASON: *Spring, summer.*

SPACING: *3 in (7.5 cm).*

ROOT DEPTH: *18 in (46 cm) and more.*

BREADTH AT MATURITY: *6–12 in (15–30 cm).*

HEIGHT AT MATURITY: *12–36 in (30–91 cm).*

SEED TO HARVEST: *20 weeks.*

SPRING PLANTING: *Plant seeds indoors 10 weeks before last frost. Transplant outdoors 4 weeks before last frost. Plant seeds outdoors 4 weeks before last frost.*

AUTUMN PLANTING: *Plant seeds indoors 16 weeks before first frost. Transplant outdoors 12 weeks before first frost.*

PH REQUIREMENT: *6.0–7.5.*

SUNLIGHT REQUIREMENT: *Full sun.*

INITIAL FERTILIZER: *Moderate nitrogen, phosphorus and potassium.*

WATER REQUIREMENT: *Medium; none for one week before harvest.*

PESTS/DISEASES: *Onion fly, thrips; downy mildew, neck rot, pink rot, smut.*

HARVEST: *For salad onions, when less than 1 in (2.5 cm) in diameter; for main crop onions, when tops fall on their own, begin checking for when bulbs pull out easily.*

PARSLEY

Petroselinum crispum

Umbelliferae, Parsley Family

GROWING SEASON: *Year-round.*

SPACING: *6 in (15 cm).*

ROOT DEPTH: *6 in (15 cm) and more.*

BREADTH AT MATURITY: *6–9 in (15–23 cm).*

HEIGHT AT MATURITY: *12–18 in (30–46 cm).*

SEED TO HARVEST: *14 weeks.*

SPRING PLANTING: *Plant seeds indoors 12 weeks before last frost. Transplant outdoors 6 weeks before last frost.*

PH REQUIREMENT: *6.0–7.0.*

SUNLIGHT REQUIREMENT: *Full to partial sun.*

INITIAL FERTILIZER: *High nitrogen.*

IN-SEASON FERTILIZER: *Every 4–6 weeks.*

WATER REQUIREMENT: *Low.*

PESTS/DISEASES: *Mildew.*

SPECIAL ATTENTION: *Usually goes to seed in second year and needs to be replanted.*

HARVEST: *As needed, as soon as leaves are large enough.*

PEAS

Pisum sativum

Leguminosae, Pea Family

GROWING SEASON: *Spring, autumn.*

SPACING: *3 in (7.5 cm).*

ROOT DEPTH: *6 in (15 cm) and more.*

BREADTH AT MATURITY: *6–10 in (15–25 cm).*

HEIGHT AT MATURITY: *2–6 ft (60–183 cm).*

SEED TO HARVEST: *10 weeks.*

SPRING PLANTING: *Plant seeds outdoors 6 weeks before last frost.*

AUTUMN PLANTING: *Plant seeds outdoors 10 weeks before first frost.*

PH REQUIREMENT: *6.0–7.5.*

SUNLIGHT REQUIREMENT: *Partial sun.*

INITIAL FERTILIZER: *Moderate phosphorus and potassium.*

IN-SEASON FERTILIZER: *When about 6 in (15 cm) tall.*

WATER REQUIREMENT: *Low; heavy after blossoms.*

PESTS/DISEASES: *Aphids, cabbage moth, bacterial blight, powdery mildew, root rot.*

SPECIAL ATTENTION: *Fragile roots; inoculate with Rhizobia bacteria before planting; if plant is not producing well, pinch off the growing tip; excellent compost material.*

HARVEST: *Before pods begin to harden and fade.*

PEPPER

Capsicum annuum

Solanaceae, Nightshade Family

GROWING SEASON: *Summer.*

SPACING: *12 in (30 cm).*

ROOT DEPTH: *8 in (20 cm) and more.*

BREADTH AT MATURITY: *24 in (60 cm).*

HEIGHT AT MATURITY: *2–3 ft (60–91 cm).*

SEED TO HARVEST: *19 weeks.*

SPRING PLANTING: *Start seeds indoors 8 weeks before last frost. Transplant outside 2 weeks after last frost.*

PH REQUIREMENT: *5.5–7.0.*

SUNLIGHT REQUIREMENT: *Full sun.*

INITIAL FERTILIZER: *Low nitrogen, phosphorus and potassium.*

IN-SEASON FERTILIZER: *When blossoms appear and 3 weeks later.*

WATER REQUIREMENT: *Medium, heavy in hot, dry periods.*

PESTS/DISEASES: *Aphids, leafminers, anthracnose, bacterial spot, blossom-end rot, mosaic.*

SPECIAL ATTENTION: *Don't over-supplement natural water; a weak spray of Epsom salt in water at blossom time will enhance fruit production.*

HARVEST: *Pick as soon as the fruits are large enough for use.*

POTATO

Solanum tuberosum

Solanaceae, Nightshade Family

GROWING SEASON: *Spring, summer.*

SPACING: *12 in (30 cm).*

ROOT DEPTH: *18 in (46 cm) and more.*

BREADTH AT MATURITY: *24 in (60 cm).*

HEIGHT AT MATURITY: *24–30 in (60–76 cm).*

SEED TO HARVEST: *15 weeks.*

SPRING PLANTING: *Plant seed potatoes outdoors 4 weeks before last frost.*

PH REQUIREMENT: *5.0–6.0.*

SUNLIGHT REQUIREMENT: *Full sun.*

INITIAL FERTILIZER: *Moderate nitrogen; high phosphorus and potassium.*

IN-SEASON FERTILIZER: *Compost only during season.*

WATER REQUIREMENT: *Medium; heavy after blossoms.*

PESTS/DISEASES: *Aphids, cabbage moths, leafhoppers, leafminers, potato tuber worms, blight, verticillium wilt, scab.*

SPECIAL ATTENTION: *Potatoes are very susceptible to disease; use disease-resistant varieties.*

HARVEST: *For new potatoes, during the blossoming period (10 weeks after planting). For main crop potatoes, after plants have died.*

RADISH

Raphanus sativus

Brassicaceae, Mustard Family

GROWING SEASON: *Spring, summer, autumn.*

SPACING: *3 in (7.5 cm).*

ROOT DEPTH: *4 in (10 cm) and more.*

BREADTH AT MATURITY: *3–8 in (7.5–10 cm).*

HEIGHT AT MATURITY: *6–12 in (15–30 cm).*

SEED TO HARVEST: *4 weeks.*

SPRING PLANTING: *Plant seeds outdoors 4 weeks before last frost.*

STAGGERED PLANTING: *Every week.*

PH REQUIREMENT: *5.5–7.0.*

SUNLIGHT REQUIREMENT: *Partial sun.*

INITIAL FERTILIZER: *Moderate nitrogen, phosphorus and potassium.*

WATER REQUIREMENT: *Moderate, to avoid hot taste.*

PESTS/DISEASES: *Cabbage moth, flea beetles, onion fly, small white, large white.*

HARVEST: *Before 1 in (2.5 cm) in diameter.*

SPINACH

Spinacia oleracea

Chenopodiaceae, Goosefoot Family

GROWING SEASON: *Spring, autumn, winter.*

SPACING: *4 in (10 cm).*

ROOT DEPTH: *12 in (30 cm) and more.*

BREADTH AT MATURITY: *6–8 in (15–20 cm).*

HEIGHT AT MATURITY: *4–8 in (10–20 cm).*

SEED TO HARVEST: *7 weeks.*

SPRING PLANTING: *Plant seeds outdoors 6 weeks before last frost.*

AUTUMN PLANTING: *Plant seeds outdoors 8 weeks before first frost.*

STAGGERED PLANTING: *2 and 4 weeks after initial planting, no more.*

PH REQUIREMENT: 6.0–7.5.

SUNLIGHT REQUIREMENT: *Partial sun.*

INITIAL FERTILIZER: *Moderate potassium.*

IN-SEASON FERTILIZER: *About 4 weeks after planting and every 2 weeks thereafter.*

WATER REQUIREMENT: *Low.*

PESTS/DISEASES: *Aphids, leafminers, whiteflies; blight, downy mildew.*

SPECIAL ATTENTION: *Spinach is quick to bolt when daylight hours increase to more than 14 per day; consider bolt-resistant varieties. New Zealand sprawls readily.*

HARVEST: *As soon as outside leaves are large enough to eat.*

SQUASH – COURGETTE

Cucurbita spp.

Cucurbitaceae, Cucumber Family

GROWING SEASON: *Summer.*

SPACING: *18 in (46 cm).*

ROOT DEPTH: *18 in (46 cm) and more.*

BREADTH AT MATURITY: *20 in (51 cm), if grown vertically.*

HEIGHT AT MATURITY: *2–5 ft (60–152 cm).*

SEED TO HARVEST: *8 weeks.*

SPRING PLANTING: *Start seeds indoors 4 weeks before last frost. Transplant outdoors on date of last frost.*

AUTUMN PLANTING: *Plant seeds or transplants outdoors 6 weeks after last spring frost.*

PH REQUIREMENT: 6.0–7.5.

SUNLIGHT REQUIREMENT: *Full sun.*

INITIAL FERTILIZER: *Moderate nitrogen, high phosphorus.*

IN-SEASON FERTILIZER: *Every 4 weeks.*

WATER REQUIREMENT: *High.*

PESTS/DISEASES: *Cabbage moth, anthracnose, bacterial wilt, downy mildew, mosaic, powdery mildew, scab.*

SPECIAL ATTENTION: *Bee pollination is crucial.*

HARVEST: *Cut before fruit is 8 in (20 cm) long.*

SQUASH – MARROW

Cucurbita spp.

Cucurbitaceae, Cucumber Family

GROWING SEASON: *Summer.*

SPACING: *18 in (46 cm).*

ROOT DEPTH: *18 in (46 cm) and more.*

BREADTH AT MATURITY: *20 in (51 cm), if grown vertically.*

HEIGHT AT MATURITY: *2–5 ft (61–154 cm).*

SEED TO HARVEST: *12 weeks.*

SPRING PLANTING: *Plant seeds outdoors 2 weeks after last frost.*

PH REQUIREMENT: *6.0–7.5.*

SUNLIGHT REQUIREMENT: *Full sun.*

INITIAL FERTILIZER: *Moderate nitrogen, high phosphorus.*

IN-SEASON FERTILIZER: *Every 4 weeks.*

WATER REQUIREMENT: *High.*

PESTS/DISEASES: *Cabbage moth, anthracnose, bacterial wilt, downy mildew, mosaic, powdery mildew, scab.*

SPECIAL ATTENTION: *Bee pollination is crucial.*

HARVEST: *Cut before fruit is 8 in (20 cm) long.*

SWEET POTATO

Ipomoea batatas

Convolvulaceae, Morning Glory Family

GROWING SEASON: *Summer.*

SPACING: *12 in (30 cm).*

ROOT DEPTH: *12 in (30 cm) and more.*

BREADTH AT MATURITY: *4–8 ft (122–244 cm).*

HEIGHT AT MATURITY: *12–15 in (30–38 cm).*

SEED TO HARVEST: *19 weeks.*

SPRING PLANTING: *Start seed potatoes indoors 1 week after last frost. Transplant outdoors 4 weeks after last frost.*

PH REQUIREMENT: *5.0–6.0.*

SUNLIGHT REQUIREMENT: *Full sun.*

INITIAL FERTILIZER: *Moderate nitrogen and phosphorus, high potassium.*

IN-SEASON FERTILIZER: *When plants take root.*

WATER REQUIREMENT: *Low.*

PESTS/DISEASES: *Flea beetles, nematodes, wireworms; black rot, soil rot.*

SPECIAL ATTENTION: *Mound soil around plants to enhance size of tubers.*

HARVEST: *As close to first autumn frost as possible, but definitely before it occurs.*

SWISS CHARD

Beta vulgaris

Chenopodisceae, Goosefoot Family

GROWING SEASON: *Year-round.*

SPACING: *6 in (15 cm).*

ROOT DEPTH: *6 in (15 cm) and more.*

BREADTH AT MATURITY: *6–10 in (15–25 cm).*

HEIGHT AT MATURITY: *8–14 in (20–36 cm).*

SEED TO HARVEST: *8 weeks.*

SPRING PLANTING: *Start seeds indoors 8 weeks before last frost. Transplant outdoors 3 weeks before last frost. Plant seeds outdoors 2 weeks before last frost.*

PH REQUIREMENT: *6.0–7.5*

SUNLIGHT REQUIREMENT: *Full to partial sun.*

INITIAL FERTILIZER: *Moderate nitrogen.*

IN-SEASON FERTILIZER: *Every 6 weeks.*

WATER REQUIREMENT: *Heavy.*

PESTS/DISEASES: *Aphids, flea beetles, leafminers, slugs, snails; blight, downy mildew.*

HARVEST: *When outer leaves are 6–8 in (15–20 cm) tall.*

TOMATO

Lycopersicon escutentum

Solanaceae, Nightshade Family

GROWING SEASON: *Summer.*

SPACING: *2 ft (60 cm).*

ROOT DEPTH: *8 in (20 cm) and more.*

BREADTH AT MATURITY: *24–36 in (60–91 cm), if grown vertically.*

HEIGHT AT MATURITY: *Determinate, 3–4 ft (91–122 cm); indeterminate, 7–15 ft (2.1–4.5 m).*

SEED TO HARVEST: *17 weeks.*

SPRING PLANTING: *Start seeds indoors 8 weeks before last frost. Transplant outdoors on date of last frost.*

PH REQUIREMENT: *5.8–7.0.*

SUNLIGHT REQUIREMENT: *Full sun.*

INITIAL FERTILIZER: *High nitrogen and phosphorus, moderate potassium.*

IN-SEASON FERTILIZER: *Every 2–3 weeks.*

WATER REQUIREMENT: *Medium.*

PESTS/DISEASES: *Aphids, cabbage moth, leafhoppers, nematodes, anthracnose, bacterial canker, blight, blossom-end rot, fusarium wilt, mosaics, payllid yellows, septoria leaf spot.*

SPECIAL ATTENTION: *Even watering is crucial from blossoms to harvest.*

HARVEST: *Pick fruit while it is evenly red and firm.*

Appendix A – Using the Zone Maps

These zone maps are an aid for those inspired readers who may wish to introduce the plants featured in this book into their own gardens.

If you can determine that the desired plant overwinters outside in the garden where you have seen it, you should be able to identify both the zone where it is growing and the zone where you live. Bearing in mind that in the smallest garden the same plant can succeed in one corner yet die in another, use of the zone maps should at least allow you to determine whether a trial with the desired plants is worthwhile.

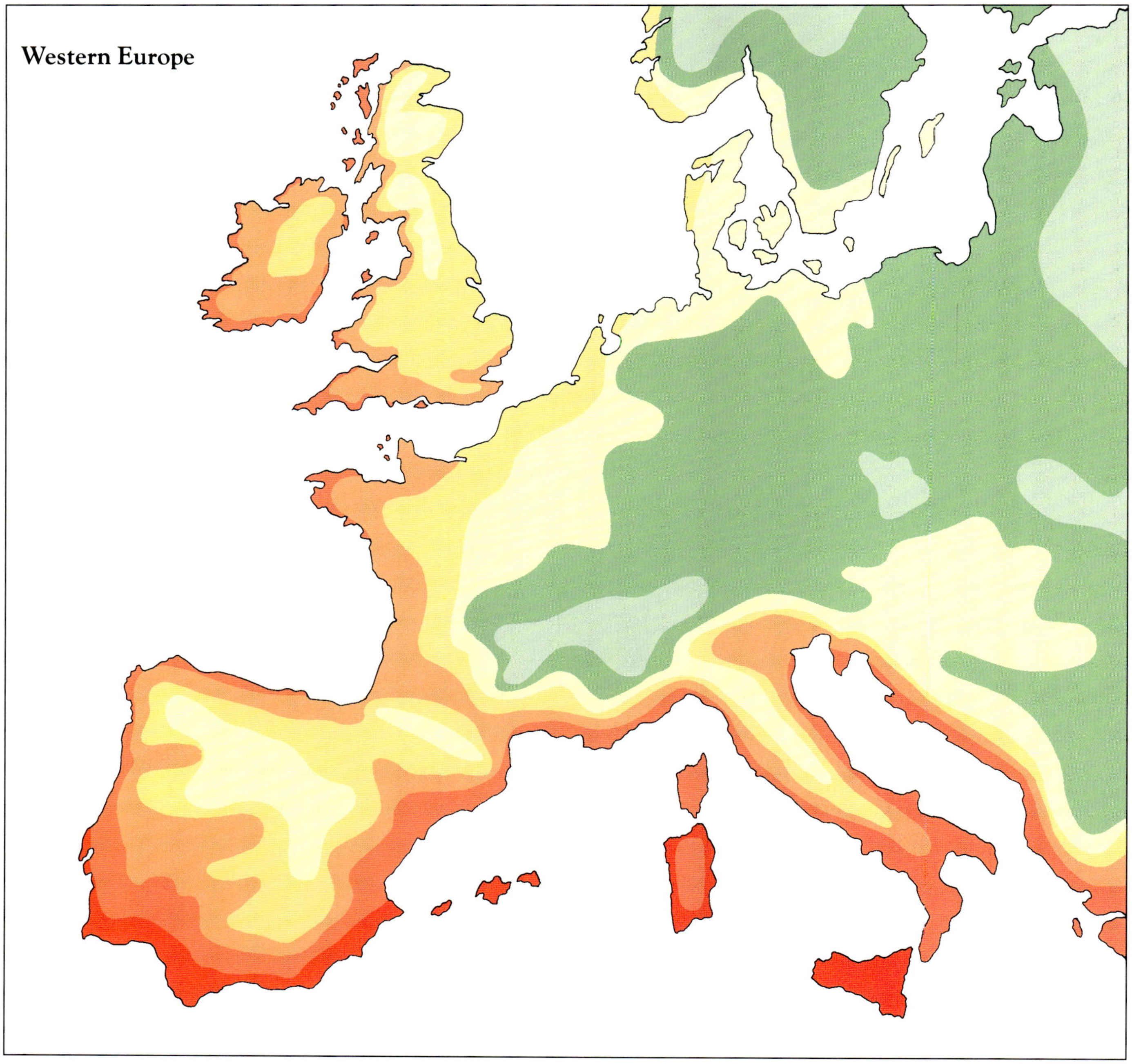

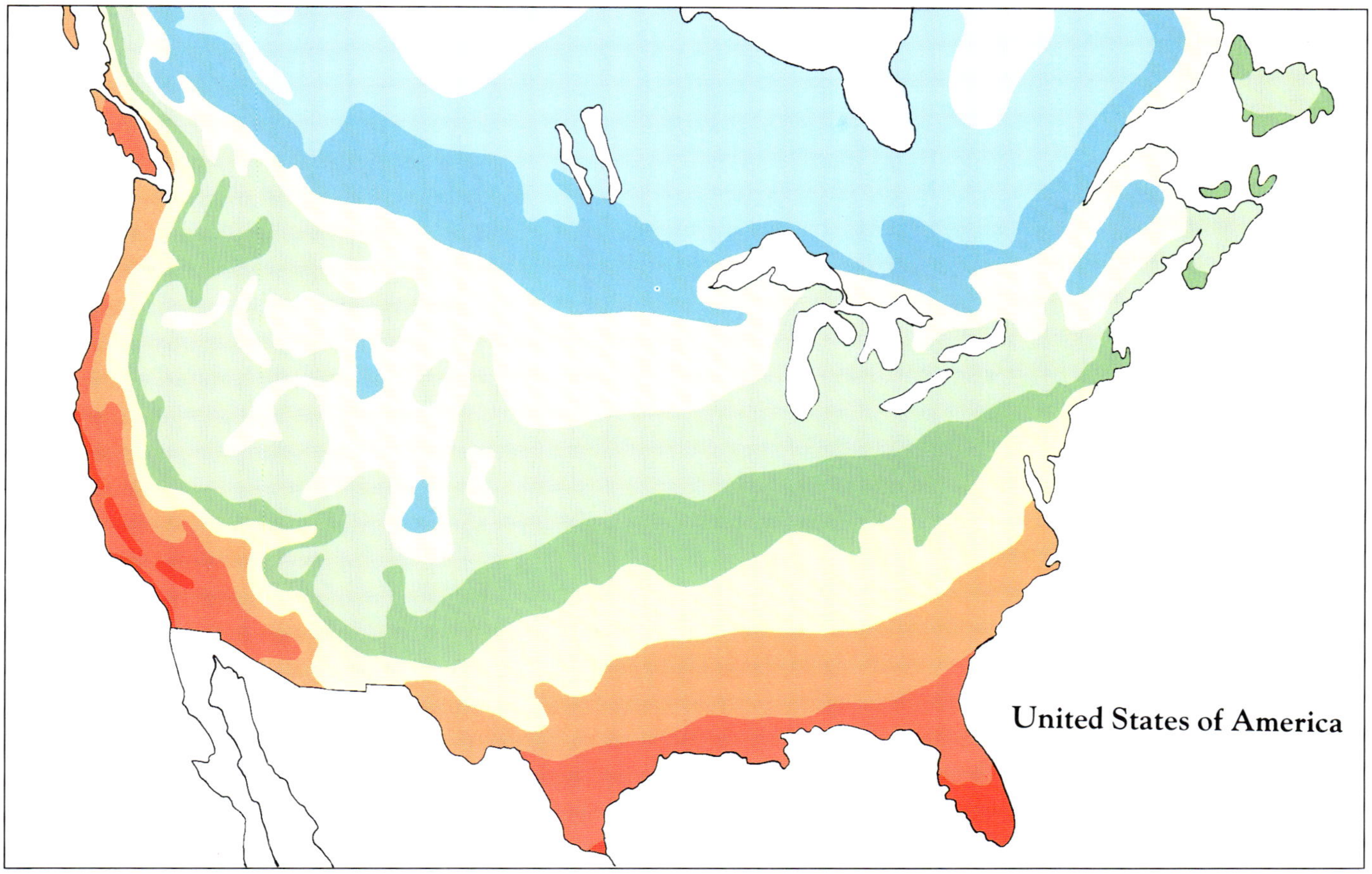

Zone 1	*below −45°C*	*below −50°F*
Zone 2	*−45°C to −40°C*	*−50°F to −40°F*
Zone 3	*−40°C to −34°C*	*−40°F to −30°F*
Zone 4	*−34°C to −29°C*	*−30°F to −20°F*
Zone 5	*−29°C to −23°C*	*−20°F to −10°F*
Zone 6	*−23°C to −18°C*	*−10°F to 0°F*
Zone 7	*−18°C to −15°C*	*0°F to 5°F*
Zone 7.5	*−15°C to −12°C*	*5°F to 10°F*
Zone 8	*−12°C to −6°C*	*10°F to 20°F*
Zone 9	*−6°C to −1°C*	*20°F to 30°F*
Zone 10	*−1°C to 5°C*	*30°F to 40°F*

Zone Key

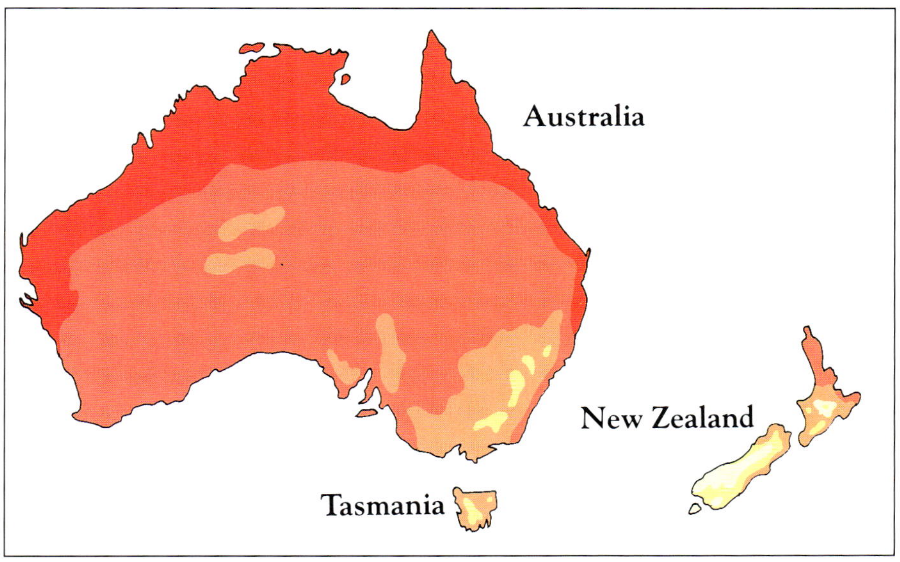

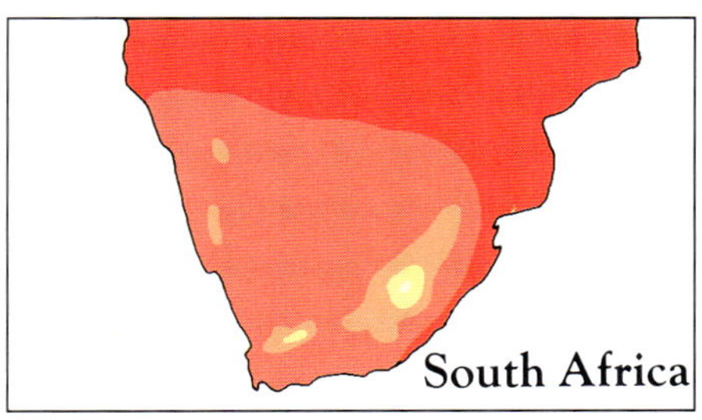

Zones designate the lowest range of temperatures that a plant will normally survive. Thus a plant in zone 9 will normally survive between −6°C and −1°C (20°F and 30°F). If a plant has been given a zone rating not shown in this key, for example 9.5, it suggests that it will survive only at the higher end of range 9 i.e. −3°C and −1°C (25°F and 30°F).

Appendix B – Container Growing

Many of the principles outlined throughout this book can be applied directly to the container-raising of crops with success. As a matter of fact, the techniques here should increase the harvest of any container effort.

Most important in container gardening is the use of an extremely high-quality soil. Normal potting soil should make up only about a quarter of the mix in each container. Your regular garden soil should never be used in containers; it will dry out and harden much too quickly.

For optimum container soil, mix one part potting soil to two parts humus and one part vermiculite. Add whatever amounts of fertilizer are appropriate to the size of the container.

Plan to water and fertilize container crops about twice as much as the same plants if they were garden-grown. In the container the soil is going to dry out very quickly, necessitating the additional waterings. And, with the extra waterings, you're going to be flushing a great deal of nutrients from your soil.

Some crops that can be successfully brought to harvest in outdoor containers are:

Aubergine: Use a container that is at least 12 in (30 cm) deep and will hold at least 5 gall (19 l) of soil; one plant per container.

Beans: Use a container that is at least 12 in (30 cm) deep and will hold at least ½ gall (2 l) of soil; one plant per container.

Beetroot: Use a container that is at least 8 in (20 cm) deep; plant as per our plant directory; harvest when no larger than 3 in (7.5 cm) in diameter.

Broccoli: Use a container that is at least 20 in (50 cm) deep and will hold 3 gall (11.3 l) of soil; one plant per container.

Cabbage: Use a container that is at least 12 in (30 cm) deep and will hold 2 gall (7.5 l) of soil; one plant per container.

Carrots: Use a container that is at least 8 in (20 deep; plant as per our plant directory.

Courgette: Use a container that is at least 24 in (60 cm) deep and will hold 5 gall (19 l) of soil; one plant per container.

Cucumbers: Use a container that is at least 10 in (25 cm) deep and will hold 2 gall (7.5 l) of soil; one plant per container.

Lettuce (salad bowl): Use a container that is at least 6 in (15 cm) deep and will hold at least a half-quart of soil; one plant per container.

Melons: Use a container that is at least 24 in (60 cm) deep and will hold at least 5 gall (19 l) of soil; one plant per container.

Onions (salad): Use a container that is at least 6 in (15 cm) deep and will hold 1 gall (3.8 l) of soil; plant as per our plant directory.

Parsley: Use a container that is at least 6 in (15 cm) deep; plant as per our plant directory.

Peas: Use a container that is at least 12 in (30 cm) deep and will hold 1 quart of soil; one plant per container.

Peppers: Use a container that is 12 in (30 cm) deep and will hold 2 gall (7.5 l) of soil; one plant per container.

Radishes: Use a container that is at least 5 in (12.7 cm) deep; plant as per our plant directory.

Spinach: Use a container that is at least 6 in (15cm) deep and will hold 1 gall (3.8 l) of soil; one plant per container.

Swiss chard: Use a container that is at least 8 in (20 cm) deep and will hold 2 gall (7.5 l) of soil; one plant per container.

Tomatoes: Use a container that is at least 12 in (30 cm) deep and will hold at least 1½ gall (5.7 l) of soil; one plant per container.

INDEX

Page numbers in *italics* refer to illustrations.

Picture credits

b = bottom, t = top, l = left, r = right, m = middle

Doris Brookes; Dwight Kuhn; **6** Paul Murphy; **7** Wayne Floyd; **8** Martin R Jones; **9** *t* Priscilla P Connell, *b* Unicorn Stock Photos; **10** William H Allen, Jr **11** *t* Martha McBride, *b* Dick Mermon **13** *t* Joan Bushno, *b* Charles Schmidt; **15** *t* Karen Holsinger Mullen, *b* Tom Fesely **16** Dwight Kuhn; **18** John Ward; **19** *t* Martha McBride; **20** *t* Jean Higgins, *b* Martha McBride; **21** *t* Martha McBride, *b* Doris Brookes; **22** B L Fegely; **23** *l* Travis Evans, *m* W Cortesi; **24** D & I MacDonald; **26** *t* Karen Holsinger Mullen, *b* Marie Mills/David Cummings; **27** Joel Dexter; **28** C A Schmeiser; **29** *t* Joel Dexter; **30** Dwight Kuhn; **32** *t* W Cortesi; **33** *l* Dwight Kuhn; **35** Dick Young; **36** *t* Joel Dexter, *b* Martha McBride; **37** *t, l* Betts Anderson, **39** Arni Katz; **40** *t* Dwight Kuhn; **41** Doris Brookes; **42** Betts Anderson; **46** *t* Dwight Kuhn, *b* M Gustafson; **47** Dwight Kuhn; **49** Joel Dexter; **50** *t* Ronald Partis, *b* Dwight Kuhn; **52** Dwight Kuhn; **53** *t* Dwight Kuhn, *m, b* Wildlife Matters; **54** Wildlife Matters; **55** W Cortesi, *t, m* Dwight Kuhn, *b* Wildlife Matters; **56** Maslowski Photo; **57** *t* Dwight Kuhn, *b* Martin Jones; **58** Eric Berndt; **59** Tom Fegely; **60** *r* Dwight Kuhn; **61** *l* Dwight Kuhn; **62** Eric Barndt, Dwight Kuhn; **63** Dwight Kuhn; **64** *l* Dwight Kuhn; **65** Martha McBride, Eric Berndt; **66** *l* Martha McBride, **68** Eric Berndt, Kimberly Burnham; **69** *l* Dwight Kuhn; **71** Dwight Kuhn, Unicorn Stock Photos; **72** William H Allen, Jr, Charles Schmidt; **73** Dwight Kuhn, Aneal Vohra; **74** Dede Gilman, Doris Brookes; **75** William H Allen Jr.

Where not specified, pictures supplied by Marcus Schneck.